Islam
Teacher Guide

Stella Neal
Series Editor: Janet Dyson
Consultant: Robert Bowie

OXFORD
UNIVERSITY PRESS

Contents

Scheme of Work

This table shows links to themes in RE across the six faiths in the *Living Faiths* series, so that you can easily navigate through the series and teach by religion or by theme. The themes are organized alphabetically under the two headings, **Beliefs** and **Moral and Ethical Issues**.

	Buddhism	Christianity	Hinduism	Islam	Judaism	Sikhism
Beliefs						
Faith origins	Overview, 1.1	Overview	Overview, 2.1	Overview	Overview	Overview
Festivals / Celebrations	2.5, 2.6	3.5, 5.2	3.2, 3.3		2.6, 3.4, 3.5, 3.7	2.6, 3.4, 3.5
Food	5.4		4.4, 4.5	3.3, 3.5	3.2	3.6, 3.7
God / Divine		1.1, 1.2, 1.3, 1.4	1.1, 1.2, 4.6	1.2	1.1, 1.3	1.1, 1.2
Key teachings	1.3, 1.4, 2.3, 2.4, 3.4	1.3, 1.6, 2.2, 4.4, 4.7	1.3, 1.4, 1.6, 3.1, 3.4, 3.5, 4.1	1.1, 1.3, 1.5, 3.1, 3.2, 3.3, 3.4	1.2, 1.4, 1.5, 2.2, 2.5	1.3, 1.4
Life after death	1.6, 2.6	2.5, 2.6	1.3	4.1, 4.2	4.2, 4.3	1.4
Places of worship	2.7	2.5, 3.2	2.5	2.5, 3.4	3.3	3.3
Religious leaders	4.3, 5.5, 5.6	2.3	1.5, 2.4, 2.5, 3.1, 4.2	2.2, 2.3	1.5, 2.7	2.1, 2.2, 2.3, 2.4
Religious symbols / Dress	1.5, 3.3	3.1	2.1	3.6	3.6	3.1, 3.2
Sacred texts	2.1, 2.2	2.1, 2.2	2.2, 2.3	2.1, 2.4	2.1, 2.2, 2.3, 2.4	2.5
Worship	3.1, 3.2, 3.3, 3.5	1.5, 2.4, 3.2, 3.3, 3.4	3.2, 3.4, 3.6	1.3, 1.5, 3.1, 3.2, 3.3, 3.4	3.1, 3.3	3.3
Moral and Ethical Issues						
Environment / Animal rights	5.4	5.4	4.4, 4.6, 4.7	4.5	4.6	4.2
Evil and suffering	1.3, 1.4	4.3, 4.5	4.2, 4.3	4.3, 4.4	4.5	5.2
Fair trade	4.4	5.5	5.5			
Gender and equality / Role of women	5.2		1.5, 5.4	3.6, 5.2	5.3	5.4
Interfaith	4.3	5.6	5.6	2.2, 5.6	5.5	5.6
Medical ethics	3.6	4.2	4.2	5.4	4.1	4.4, 4.5
Relationships / Marriage / Family	5.2	5.2, 5.3	3.3, 5.3	5.2, 5.3	5.1, 5.2	4.6
Science and religion	4.5	4.1		4.6, 5.4		4.3
Secular and atheist worldviews	4.5		1.1, 1.6	5.5	4.4, 5.5	4.3
War and peace	4.2, 5.5, 5.6	4.5, 4.6	3.1, 4.2, 5.5	4.3	5.5	5.2, 5.5
Wealth / Poverty / Charity	5.3	5.1, 5.6	3.1, 5.1	3.2	5.4	3.6, 3.8, 4.1

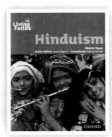

Introduction to *Living Faiths*

 How we live now

Living Faiths draws on the rich heritage of culture and diversity in twenty-first century Britain. The series focuses on case studies (shown through film and print) of young people and their families in the UK who describe how their faith affects the way they live and the moral and ethical decisions they make. The emphasis is on the personal significance of religious faith, exploring the question: What does it *mean* to be a Buddhist, Christian, Hindu, Jew, Muslim or Sikh?

This approach allows students to experience the subject fully and see its relevance to their own lives. Engagement with the case study families creates awareness of diversity, encouraging respect and enhancing social awareness. Hearing and seeing young people sharing their faith and aspects of their daily lives helps students clarify their own perspectives and reflect on their experiences, build their sense of identity and belonging, challenge prejudices and provide the knowledge and understanding to enable them to flourish in their communities.

 Flexible and adaptable

Living Faiths is a series of six books, teacher guides and online resources covering Buddhism, Christianity, Hinduism, Islam, Judaism, and Sikhism. The series is designed to allow teachers the flexibility to teach by faiths or by themes, and the Scheme of Work (on page 3) provides guidance at a glance on how to teach by themes. Through structured questioning and activities, students are encouraged to make links as they learn about a range of faiths and secular world views. They are expected to identify similarities and differences within faiths, and the *Teacher Guide* further provides suggestions on how to compare and contrast between faiths. There is a strong emphasis on sources including sacred texts, film interviews, audio and music

to give students access to the lived experience of the case study families and learn what their faith means in practice.

 Pedagogy

The series takes a mixed pedagogical approach inspired by the important ethnographic work that has been developed in RE in recent years. Throughout the series students are introduced to the study of faith as it is practised by believers today. The enquiry-driven focus enables them to engage with the voices and personalities of faith, getting beyond generalizations and over-simplifications, to enter into dialogue with people about their faith. Through this dialogue with living faith students will be encouraged to reflect on the experiences and beliefs of others and also on their own experiences of faith, belief and what really matters in life.

The *Living Faiths* series has been designed to engage, interest and challenge students. Each unit has an intriguing title, often a question, to capture the interest of students as soon as the lesson begins. The 'starter' activities get students thinking and discussing, drawing on their prior learning or their personal experiences as ways into the main lesson focus.

 Questioning

Questioning is fundamental to good teaching and learning. Higher order questions enable students to tackle issues at a deep level and extend their thinking, develop independence in the way they learn and think and come to a fuller understanding of an idea because they have tried to explain it themselves. Bloom's Taxonomy (1956), is a useful tool for planning sequences of different types of questions of increasing difficulty to promote higher order thinking. Many of the activities are designed for pair and group discussion or for independent and small group research to promote student participation. Through the activities students will develop the ability to speculate, to raise their own questions and seek answers for themselves.

Reflection

Which would you prefer: to follow a clear set of requirements, or to do things your own way? Why?

Activities

1. Write a postcard to Ibrahim Yassin, above, asking him questions about the Five Pillars and what they mean to him. Create a relevant design on the other side.

2. Which personal qualities would a Muslim have if he or she followed the Five Pillars? How else could these qualities be developed? Discuss with a partner.

3. 'People should be allowed to worship in any way they wish.' How would you respond to this comment? Consider arguments for and against.

4. Can you think of 'pillars' in your own life? Something: you give; you always remember; you want to do once in your life; you do every year; you do several times a day.

The activities are colour coded to identify three modes of thinking that are particularly valuable in the study of religion, philosophy and the broad area of social sciences.

Students are encouraged to:

- **Red: 'Think like a theologian'** these questions focus on understanding the nature of religious belief, its symbolism and spiritual significance; in the *Student Book* they are highlighted by a red question number

- **Blue: 'Think like a philosopher'** these questions focus on analysing and debating big ideas such as truth and reality; in the *Student Book* they are highlighted by a blue question number

- **Green: 'Think like a social scientist'** these questions focus on exploring and analysing why people do what they do and how belief affects action; in the *Student Book* they are highlighted by a green question number

 Reflection

Reflection helps students to deepen their thinking and apply their learning about the religious beliefs and practices of others. It encourages them to explore their own beliefs in the light of what they learn, whether they are religious or not, and how they impact on personal ethics.

 Thinking skills

In RE students are expected to think in increasing depth about complex issues to do with faith, beliefs, ideas and motivation. Philosophical enquiry-based approaches such as mind-mapping help students to think creatively, analytically and critically; to listen to, evaluate and respond to the views and ideas of others; to give reasons for their opinions, make connections and hypothesize; to give both sides of an argument, evaluate and draw conclusions.

Assessment

At the end of each unit there is a final assessment task which draws together students' learning.

Assessment for learning strategies are built into every unit:

- Learning objectives for each unit are written in student-friendly language and shared with students
- Students know what standards and levels they are aiming for
- Self- and peer-assessment opportunities are supported by 'I can' statements
- **AT1 Learning *about* religion** is assessed using auto-marked tests to help save you time setting questions and marking
- **AT2 Learning *from* religion** is assessed with step-by-step tasks and support materials. These use effective assessment for learning strategies to help students recognize next steps and improve performance.

We hope that you will enjoy using this series to bring real families of faith into the classroom, and to introduce students to the liveliness and relevance of religious education.

Janet Dyson
(Series Editor)

Robert Bowie
(Series Consultant)

About this Series

Living Faiths Islam is one of six Religious Education Student Books covering the following major faiths: Buddhism, Christianity, Hinduism, Islam, Judaism, and Sikhism. This series fully integrates real-life film clips and other exciting multimedia resources on *Kerboodle* with the *Student Books* and *Teacher Guides*, so your lessons can be delivered easily and seamlessly.

The series components

The series consist of:

For students

- Six *Student Books* (and/or six *Kerboodle Books*)
- Six *Kerboodle* Lessons, Resources and Assessments.

For teachers

- Six *Teacher Guides*
- Six *Kerboodle* Lessons, Resources and Assessments (includes teacher access to the accompanying *Kerboodle Book*).

 Student Book

The ***Living Faiths Islam Student Book*** uses **real-life case studies** to encourage students to ask questions, actively engage with **moral** and **ethical** issues, and reflect on the relevance of RE.

> Starter activities spark your students' interest in new topics

> The 'Reflection' feature helps your students to consider beliefs and practices of others, and how they link to their own lives and beliefs

Islam Student Book

> Colour-coded activities develop varied skills and are structured to encourage progression and allow differentiation

Case studies provide first-hand experience of real Muslim families talking about their faith

Islam Student Book

There is an assessment spread for every chapter in the *Student Book* to help students determine what level they are aiming for and make progress

Extensions tasks within assessments challenge more able students

Case studies are linked directly to films on *Kerboodle* and are marked with film icons on each page

Authors

Experienced RE Consultant **Janet Dyson** and well-known author and PGCE tutor **Robert Bowie** lead the author **Stella Neal**, who is an experienced RE teacher.

Islam Kerboodle

Using this Book

 Teacher Guide

The *Living Faiths Islam Teacher Guide* aims to save you time and effort. It provides **full support** and guidance for the *Islam Student Book*, including **practical tasks** and **creative suggestions** for incorporating differentiation into your teaching.

What it provides

For each chapter of the student book, this book provides:

- a chapter overview
- help at a glance for each unit
- further suggestions for class and homework
- an assessment overview.

It also has a **Glossary** at the back, covering the RE terms students will meet.

Please turn to the **Contents List** on page 2 to see how this book is structured. While the Living Faiths series is organized by religion, a **Scheme of Work** on page 3 is also provided to help you teach RE **by themes**.

Find out more about the four main components below.

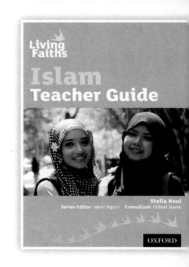

The chapter overview

This is your introduction to the corresponding *Student Book* chapter.

> Shows how the *Student Book* chapter relates to the KS3 RE Programme of Study (non-statutory)

> Reminds you that some lessons, including starters and plenaries, will need resources prepared in advance

> Sets out the key ideas within, and behind, the chapter in the *Student Book*

> Points you to the assessment material for the chapter (summative and formal assessments, and related resources)

> Gives a brief summary of what's covered in the *Student Book* chapter. It will help you give students a road map for the chapter

> Sets out the objectives and outcomes for the chapter, and the corresponding unit numbers

Help at a glance for each unit

These pages give comprehensive help for each unit of the *Student Book*.

Starts with a brief walk through the unit, to show you how it develops

Summarizes ideas covered in the unit, plus underlying ideas where appropriate

New terms introduced in the unit. See the glossary at the back of the book

A list of all the resources available on *Kerboodle* for the unit

Points you to related material on *Kerboodle*, including interactive activities, worksheets, homework ideas and assessment opportunities

Suggestions for starters

This section provides clarification and extra information for some activities in the *Student Book*

Suggests plenaries for use throughout the lesson, not just at the end

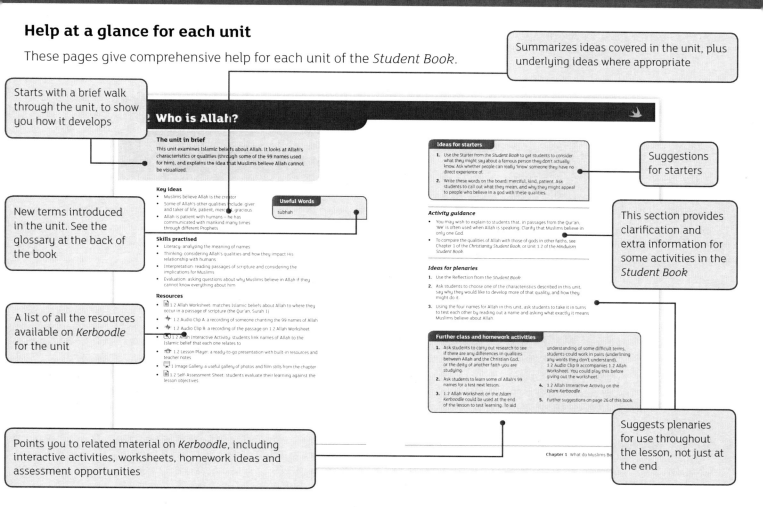

Further suggestions for class and homework

These pages give a bank of further suggestions for class and homework.

They have been graded *, ** or *** according to level of difficulty.

These suggestions are addressed directly to students.

1.1 Who are Muslims?

1 Keep a record of images from this week's media, showing – in your opinion – clothes suitable for a modern British Muslim. Make notes about each one to explain why you think the clothing is suitable. *

2 Copy and decorate the Shahadah in Arabic

1.4 How do Muslims put their Beliefs into Action from Birth?

1 What words or advice would you whisper in a baby's ear, if any? Write down your thoughts and explain your reasons. **

2 Complete a detailed research task about why Muslims like calligraphy. Consider their beliefs on the matter and present examples. Then provide your

Suggestions are graded, but some are suitable for all levels, and differentiated by outcome

The assessment overview

This section introduces you to the end-of-chapter assessment task from the *Student Book*, and describes the support materials available for the chapter.

Assessment in the *Student Book*

You will find an assessment task at the end of every chapter which focuses on AT2. In this chapter, the task asks students in groups to prepare for a debate on the statement: 'Belief in Allah is all a Muslim needs.'

In the *Student Book* (and on the supporting worksheets), you'll find guidance about levels of assessment that you can use to help your students understand what their work should include. You could ask them to use these criteria for self- or peer-assessment once they've completed the task.

Living Faiths Assessment

Student Book
- Assessment Task
- Levels Guidance

Kerboodle
- Auto-Marked Test
- Assessment Task Presentation
- Assessment Worksheets

The purpose of the end-of-chapter assessment task from the *Student Book* is summarized

You can see all the assessment materials available for the chapter at a glance

Kerboodle

Living Faiths Islam Kerboodle is packed full of guidedsupport and ideas for running and creating effective lessons on Islam. It's intuitive to use, customizable, and can be accessed online.

It consists of:

- Islam Lessons, Resources and Assessments (includes teacher access to the accompanying *Kerboodle Book*)
- *Islam Kerboodle Book*.

 ## Lessons, Resources and Assessment

Living Faiths Islam Kerboodle – Lessons, Resources and Assessment provides over one hundred lively built-in resources, including unique specially commissioned films of real Muslim families practising their faiths, interactive activities, ready-to-go lesson presentations, and supported assessment tasks. You can even **adapt** many of these resources to suit you and your students' individual needs, and **upload** your existing resources so everything can be accessed from one location. Image collections and audio clips are also included to help bring RE to life in your classroom.

Lessons, Resources and Assessment provides:

- Resources
- Lessons
- Assessment and Markbook
- Teacher access to the *Kerboodle Book*.

Find out more about the four main components below.

Resources

Click on the **Resources tab** at the top of the screen to access the full list of *Living Faiths Islam* resources.

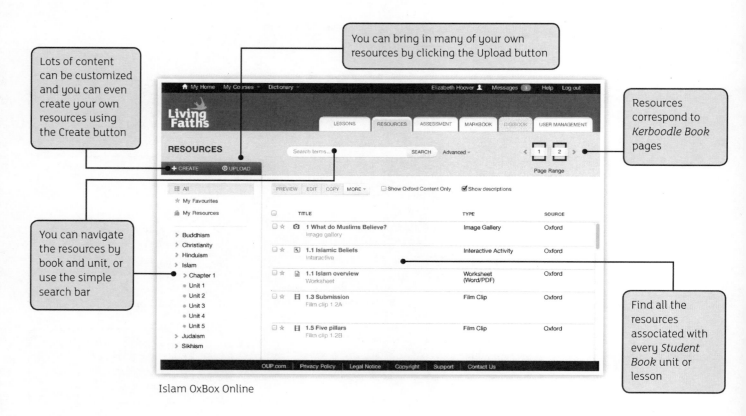

You can bring in many of your own resources by clicking the Upload button

Lots of content can be customized and you can even create your own resources using the Create button

Resources correspond to *Kerboodle Book* pages

You can navigate the resources by book and unit, or use the simple search bar

Find all the resources associated with every *Student Book* unit or lesson

Islam OxBox Online

The Resources section has more than:

 20 Film clips: Specially commissioned films help your students to actively engage with RE through watching real Muslim families practise their faith and to explore the diversity within Islam.

 10 Audio clips: Specially commissioned music and narrated sources help bring RE alive in your classroom.

 70 Worksheets: Creative worksheets that help provide differentiation/extension material for each unit, and film worksheets to help students assess their own learning of the case study film clips and link ideas back to the *Student Book* unit. They are provided as PDFs, which you can print off and photocopy, and as Word files, which you can amend to suit your students' needs.

 30 Interactive activities: Various types of activities are available for each unit as short main activities, plenaries or summative assessments. They can also be used for independent study. Most of these activities are auto-marked to help you save time marking.

 80 Images: An image gallery with captions is provided for each chapter so you can easily enlarge any photo or artwork from the *Student Book* on screen and use it as a discussion starter, use them in your own worksheets, or give them to students to use in class or homework activities.

***Kerboodle* Resources are fully integrated with the *Student Book*:**

Islam
Student Book

Real Muslim families are featured in the *Student Book* and you can find the specially commissioned films related to *Student Book* units on *Kerboodle*

Use the accompanying film worksheets to help your students consolidate what they have learnt

All the resources and assessments are **fully integrated** with the *Islam Student Book*

Kerboodle

Lesson presentations

Click on the **Lessons tab** to access the full list of *Living Faiths Islam* lessons and notes.

🏠 **Ready-to-play lesson presentations** complement every unit in the book. Each lesson presentation is easy to launch, and features unit objectives, the related starters, worksheets, film and interactive resources, and closes with a plenary activity or reflection. You can further **personalize** the lessons by adding in your own resources and notes. Your lessons and notes can be accessed by your whole department, and they are a great time-saver and **ideal for non-specialist** teachers and cover lessons.

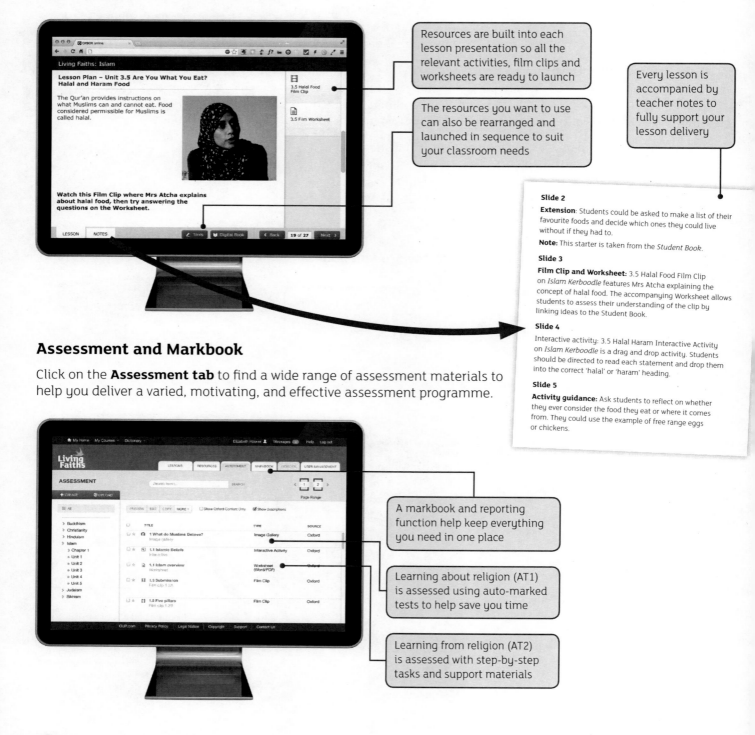

Resources are built into each lesson presentation so all the relevant activities, film clips and worksheets are ready to launch

The resources you want to use can also be rearranged and launched in sequence to suit your classroom needs

Every lesson is accompanied by teacher notes to fully support your lesson delivery

Slide 2

Extension: Students could be asked to make a list of their favourite foods and decide which ones they could live without if they had to.

Note: This starter is taken from the *Student Book*.

Slide 3

Film Clip and Worksheet: 3.5 Halal Food Film Clip on *Islam Kerboodle* features Mrs Atcha explaining the concept of halal food. The accompanying Worksheet allows students to assess their understanding of the clip by linking ideas to the Student Book.

Slide 4

Interactive activity: 3.5 Halal Haram Interactive Activity on *Islam Kerboodle* is a drag and drop activity. Students should be directed to read each statement and drop them into the correct 'halal' or 'haram' heading.

Slide 5

Activity guidance: Ask students to reflect on whether they ever consider the food they eat or where it comes from. They could use the example of free range eggs or chickens.

Assessment and Markbook

Click on the **Assessment tab** to find a wide range of assessment materials to help you deliver a varied, motivating, and effective assessment programme.

A markbook and reporting function help keep everything you need in one place

Learning about religion (AT1) is assessed using auto-marked tests to help save you time

Learning from religion (AT2) is assessed with step-by-step tasks and support materials

The Assessment section provides:

- **2 baseline tests:** These tests cover both **Attainment Target 1** (learning *about* religion) and **Attainment Target 2** (learning *from* religion), and they can help you to quickly assess the prior RE knowledge that your new KS3 students may have.

- **5 auto-marked tests**: Each end-of-chapter auto-marked test assesses **AT1**. The marks are automatically reported in the **Markbook tab**.

- **30 self-assessment worksheets**: Self-assessment worksheets help students to self- or peer-evaluate the skills they have learnt from each unit.

- **5 assessment task presentations**: Each end-of-chapter assessment task in the *Student Book*, which assesses **AT2**, has a front-of-class presentation for you to use to help guide students towards understanding and analysing what the question/task is asking of them. You can lead students through this step-by-step presentation and help them decide how to prepare to answer the question.

- **15 assessment worksheets**: These worksheets complement the assessment tasks in the *Student Book* and the assessment task presentations. They recap the task, provide a self-evaluation chart, and space for students to prepare their work.

A **Markbook** with reporting function completes the *Kerboodle* assessment package, so you can keep track of all your students' test results and assessment scores. This includes both the automarked tests and work that need to be marked by you. It is also easy to import class registers and create user accounts for all your students.

Kerboodle Book

The *Islam Kerboodle Book* provides you with an on-screen version of the *Student Book* for you to use on your whiteboard with the whole class.

Teacher access to the *Kerboodle Book* is **automatically available** as part of the Lessons, Resources and Assessment package. You can also choose to buy access for your students.

Both teacher and student access include a simple bank of tools so you can personalize the book and take notes.

It can be accessed on other devices, such as tablets.

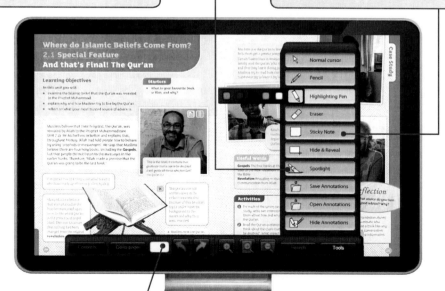

Zoom in and spotlight any part of the text

Use different tools such as Sticky Notes, Bookmarks and Pencil features to personalize each page

Navigate around the book quickly with the contents menu, keyword search or page number search

Every teacher and student has their own digital notebook for use within their *Kerboodle Book*. You can even choose to share some of your notes with your students, or hide them from view – all student notes are accessible to themselves only

Chapter 1 Overview
What do Muslims Believe?

Helping you deliver Key Stage 3 RE

This chapter addresses the following areas of the Programme of Study:

Key concepts

Beliefs, teachings and sources
- Interpreting teachings and ways of life in order to understand religions and beliefs
- Understanding and responding critically to beliefs and attitudes

Practices and ways of life
- Exploring the impact of religions and beliefs on how people live their lives

Meaning, purpose and truth
- Exploring some of the ultimate questions that confront humanity, and responding imaginatively to them

Key processes

Learning about religion
- Investigate the impact of religious beliefs and teachings on individuals and the reasons for commitment
- Apply a wide range of religious and philosophical vocabulary consistently and accurately, recognizing both the power and limitations of language in expressing religious ideas and beliefs
- Analyze religious beliefs, arguments and ideas

Learning from religion
- Reflect on the relationship between beliefs, teachings, world issues and ultimate questions

The big picture

These are the key ideas behind this chapter:

- The declaration of faith in Islam states that there is one God, Allah, and Muhammad is His Messenger.
- Allah is the creator who has been patient with humans throughout history, and has sent guidance so that humans know how to live a good life and secure eternal life with Him in heaven.
- There are five actions (pillars) that all Muslims must undertake. Living the Muslim life is about prioritizing those actions.

- Muslims try to keep Allah in mind all the time, so that they are less likely to commit sin and more likely to develop a love for Allah.
- Peace and submission are key concepts in Islam.

Chapter outline

Use this to give students a mental road map of the chapter:

1.1 Who are Muslims? – looks at what makes someone Muslim, and how one might recognize a Muslim through their behaviour and stated beliefs

1.2 Who is Allah? – explores Islamic beliefs about Allah, including the 99 names Muslims use to describe Him and His characteristics

1.3 A Whole Way of Life: Submission to Allah – examines the central role of Allah in the life of Muslims, and analyses the belief that Muslims should submit to His will

1.4 How do Muslims put their Beliefs into Action from Birth? – considers the involvement of Allah in the day-to-day lives of Muslims, and their responses to Him

1.5 What are the Five Pillars? – introduces the Five Pillars of Islam (Chapter 3 covers the pillars in more detail)

Opportunities for assessment

Baseline auto-marked test and assessment tasks are available on the *Islam Kerboodle*. This allows you to evaluate how much knowledge students already have about Islam before you start the course.

Summative assessments on the *Islam Kerboodle* include auto-marked tests, interactive activities and self-assessment worksheets.

The end-of-chapter assessment task in the *Student Book* provides formative assessment. Supporting materials for the assessment task can be found on the *Islam Kerboodle*, such as the Assessment Task Presentation and the related worksheets.

There are other opportunities for assessment too. For example, you could use some of the activities or reflection points throughout each *Student Book* unit, or some of the 'Further Suggestions' at the end of this chapter.

Getting ready for this chapter

- Before starting the course, it is important to know where students are coming from in their attitudes towards Islam, as some may be anti-Islamic. Allow students to be honest about their starting point on Islam. If students express negative views, it is helpful to suggest this course as a way of getting beyond some common misconceptions and finding out who Muslims really are.

- The study of Islam can also produce letters from parents, and it is worth considering whether your school has any specific policies or procedures to respond to matters like this before the course starts.

- You might find it useful to obtain certain artefacts, such as a poster of the Shahadah for display.

- If possible, you could arrange a visit to a local mosque at some point during the term.

- If you have the *Islam Kerboodle*, watch the case study film clips in advance, so that you can prepare and guide students before and during their viewing.

Objectives and outcomes for this chapter

Objectives	Unit	Outcomes
Most students will:		Most students will be able to:
• investigate what makes someone a Muslim • evaluate the qualities Muslims value in a person • reflect on what makes you who you are.	1.1	• describe a Muslim by their appearance, actions and beliefs • explain why certain qualities are valued • describe values that they hold and say why.
• explain some Islamic beliefs about Allah • investigate why Muslims do not draw pictures representing Allah • evaluate the difficulty of developing certain character traits.	1.2	• give and explain at least three of Allah's names • refer to Allah as infinite and unknowable and reference this to Islamic scriptures • identify situations which develop certain character traits.
• examine the belief held by many Muslims that everything comes second to their faith in Allah • explain the belief that Muslims should submit to the will of Allah • reflect on what the driving force is in their life.	1.3	• state why Muslims submit to God • give examples of what submission means in practice • say what they think about why people trust in God.
• develop an understanding of how Muslims see Allah's involvement in their daily lives from birth onwards • learn how belief in Allah turns into action • evaluate the idea that people are born with the desire to be with Allah.	1.4	• describe a ritual associated with birth; state the responsibility of Muslim parents in raising a child • explain why Muslims refer everything back to Allah • reflect on what influences them at key times in their lives.
• learn about the significance of the Five Pillars for Muslims • develop an understanding of and explain how Muslims put the Five Pillars into action • analyse why some duties are easier to follow than others.	1.5	• list the Five Pillars of Islam and explain their significance • compare the Five Pillars with their own personal 'pillars' • identify things that might get in the way of someone practising the Five Pillars.

The unit in brief

This unit looks at what makes someone Muslim. It considers stated beliefs, practices and Islamic clothing, and explores the fact that Islam has many diverse expressions. It introduces the idea that Islam comes from the Arabic word for peace.

Key ideas

- Allah is the name for God in Islam
- Many Muslims choose to wear some kind of Islamic clothing, but many do not
- The Shahadah is the Muslim declaration of faith
- Muslims believe that submitting to Allah will bring them peace

Useful Words

Allah, hijab, mosque clothes, Qur'an, Shahadah

Skills practised

- Thinking: using the Venn diagram to make links between look like/do/believe
- Communication: discussing the most important personal characteristics
- Literacy: looking at word roots and the origin of words
- Reflection: considering own beliefs and characteristics

Resources

- 📄 1.1 Islam Overview Worksheet A: students fill out a 'look like, do, believe' Venn diagram for Muslims and then themselves
- 📄 1.1 Islam Overview Worksheet B: students complete a spider diagram with key ideas about Islam throughout their studies
- 〰 1.1 Audio Clip: a recording of the Shahadah in English and Arabic
- ↖ 1.1 Islamic Beliefs Interactive Activity: students decide whether statements are true or false
- 🎓 1.1 Lesson Player: a ready-to-go presentation with built-in resources and teacher notes
- 🖼 1 Image Gallery: a useful gallery of photos and film stills from the chapter
- 📄 1.1 Self-Assessment Sheet: students evaluate their learning against the lesson objectives

Ideas for starters

1. Use the Starter from the *Student Book*. The activity asks students what words or images they associate with Muslims. It's possible that some negative words may be used, so it might be necessary to acknowledge any negative impressions and explore where they come from.

2. Ask students, in pairs, to discuss what different people might say about them from the way they look – friends, teachers, family, or strangers. Ask whether they think the reaction would depend on what they were wearing.

3. Ask students to look at the Venn diagram in the *Student Book*. Then ask them to come up with a series of interesting questions to create more words and phrases for the diagram.

Activity guidance

*   The first part of Activity 1 in the *Student Book* could form the basis of a class discussion, followed by a class vote. Students could write down their immediate response to the outcome of the class vote – do they agree and why/why not?

*   You might want to explain that Islam does not use pictures of Allah, because Muslims believe that it's not possible for a human – who was created by God – to imagine what God might look like.

Ideas for plenaries

1. Use the Reflection from the *Student Book*.

2. You could start a word wall about peace and Islam. This lesson contains the idea that doing what Allah wants can bring a Muslim peace. Ask students to include what brings them peace.

3. Ask students to reflect on a positive character trait that they would like to develop this week. Ask them how they will go about it.

4. Ask students to write a text message explaining one thing that they have learned about Muslims or Islam this lesson. It could be in the form: 'Did you know that Muslims/Islam …?'

Further class and homework activities

1. Ask students to present three arguments for, and three arguments against, showing the outward signs of one's belief.

2. You could use 1.1 Islam Overview Worksheet A on the *Islam Kerboodle* to support both the Starter and Reflection in the *Student Book*.

3. Play students 1.1 Audio Clip on the *Islam Kerboodle* and ask: 'Why do you think Muslims often repeat this to themselves and others?'

4. 1.1 Islamic Beliefs Interactive Activity on the *Islam Kerboodle*.

5. 1.1 Islam Overview Worksheet B on the *Islam Kerboodle*.

6. Further suggestions on page 26 of this book.

The unit in brief

This unit examines Islamic beliefs about Allah. It looks at Allah's characteristics or qualities (through some of the 99 names used for him), and explains the idea that Muslims believe Allah cannot be visualized.

Key ideas

- Muslims believe Allah is the creator
- Some of Allah's other qualities include: giver and taker of life, patient, merciful, gracious
- Allah is patient with humans – he has communicated with mankind many times through different Prophets

Skills practised

- Literacy: analysing the meaning of names
- Thinking: considering Allah's qualities and how they impact His relationship with humans
- Interpretation: reading passages of scripture and considering the implications for Muslims
- Evaluation: asking questions about why Muslims believe in Allah if they cannot know everything about him

Resources

- 1.2 Allah Worksheet: matches Islamic beliefs about Allah to where they occur in a passage of scripture (the Qur'an, Surah 1)
- 1.2 Audio Clip A: a recording of someone chanting the 99 names of Allah
- 1.2 Audio Clip B: a recording of the passage on 1.2 Allah Worksheet
- 1.2 Allah Interactive Activity: students link names of Allah to the Islamic belief that each one relates to
- 1.2 Lesson Player: a ready-to-go presentation with built-in resources and teacher notes
- 1 Image Gallery: a useful gallery of photos and film stills from the chapter
- 1.2 Self-Assessment Sheet: students evaluate their learning against the lesson objectives

Ideas for starters

1. Use the Starter from the *Student Book* to get students to consider what they might say about a famous person they don't actually know. Ask whether people can really 'know' someone they have no direct experience of.

2. Write these words on the board: merciful, kind, patient. Ask students to call out what they mean, and why they might appeal to people who believe in a god with these qualities.

Activity guidance

- You may wish to explain to students that, in passages from the Qur'an, 'We' is often used when Allah is speaking. Clarify that Muslims believe in only one God.

- To compare the qualities of Allah with those of gods in other faiths, see Chapter 1 of the *Christianity Student Book*, or Unit 1.2 of the *Hinduism Student Book*.

Ideas for plenaries

1. Use the Reflection from the *Student Book*.

2. Ask students to choose one of the characteristics described in this unit, say why they would like to develop more of that quality, and how they might do it.

3. Using the four names for Allah in this unit, ask students to take it in turns to test each other by reading out a name and asking what exactly it means Muslims believe about Allah.

Further class and homework activities

1. Ask students to carry out research to see if there are any differences in qualities between Allah and the Christian God, or the deity of another faith you are studying.

2. Ask students to learn some of Allah's 99 names for a test next lesson.

3. 1.2 Allah Worksheet on the *Islam Kerboodle* could be used at the end of the lesson to test learning. To aid understanding of some difficult terms, students could work in pairs (underlining any words they don't understand). 1.2 Audio Clip B accompanies 1.2 Allah Worksheet. You could play this before giving out the worksheet.

4. 1.2 Allah Interactive Activity on the *Islam Kerboodle*.

5. Further suggestions on page 26 of this book.

1.3 A Whole Way of Life: Submission to Allah

The unit in brief

This unit looks in more detail at the central role of Allah in the life of many Muslims. The idea of submitting to Allah's 'will' is considered, as well as a case study about how submission might bring peace.

Key ideas

- Muslims believe Allah is the one and only universal God
- There is nothing like Allah, so nothing is more important than Him
- The Qur'an is the Word of Allah, so Muslims follow its teachings in every aspect of their lives
- Muslims submit to Allah's will

Skills practised

- Thinking: considering the relationship between submission and peace
- Application: discussing how submission would impact daily life
- Problem solving: developing arguments about free will and submission
- Reflection: analysing why people choose to submit

Resources

- 1.3 Submission Film Clip: Mrs Yassin talks about the importance of submitting to Allah in today's society

- 1.3 Film Worksheet: students assess their understanding of the case study film clip by linking ideas to the Student Book

- 1.3 Submission Interactive Activity: students link key terms from the unit with their definitions

- 1.3 Lesson Player: a ready-to-go presentation with built-in resources and teacher notes

- 1 Image Gallery: a useful gallery of photos and film stills from the chapter

- 1.3 Self-Assessment Sheet: students evaluate their learning against the lesson objectives

Ideas for starters

1. Use the Starter from the *Student Book*.

2. Ask students to form a trust line by lining up in pairs, one behind the other (an arm's length apart). The student in front should then fall backwards to be caught by the student behind. Discuss how difficult it was for the fallers to trust the catchers.

3. Ask students to speak about a time when they really had to trust someone. Ask: 'Is there anyone you trust enough to do whatever they tell you? Explain.'

Activity guidance

- The question of free will and submission in Activity 4 in the *Student Book* may need unpacking for some students. Many Muslims believe that Allah is completely in control, but that human beings have the choice about whether or not to submit to that control. You could ask students whether 'free will' is really 'free', if the consequences of choosing not to submit are bad ones.

Ideas for plenaries

1. Use the Reflection from the *Student Book*.

2. Ask students to make a bookmark for a Muslim to use in their Qur'an that sums up the attitude they should have towards the Word of Allah.

3. Divide students into groups and ask them to discuss what kinds of authority they would submit to, and what kinds they wouldn't.

4. Ask students to add one word at a time to make a sentence to summarize the lesson.

Further class and homework activities

1. Ask students to write a letter to a Muslim explaining why they should not spend hours in prayer asking Allah for something they want. They should use the key points from the lesson.

2. Show students 1.3 Submission Film Clip on the *Islam Kerboodle*, and use 1.3 Film Worksheet to facilitate a discussion about the themes raised.

3. 1.3 Submission Interactive Activity on the *Islam Kerboodle*.

4. Further suggestions on page 26 of this book.

The unit in brief

This unit begins with the Islamic belief that all people are born with the desire to be with Allah. It looks at some of the ways in which Muslims try to keep Allah in mind, and how they put their belief in Him into action.

Key ideas

- Allah created life and everyone is born with an instinctive need for Him
- Parents have the responsibility for their child's spiritual needs
- Many Muslims acknowledge Allah regularly when they speak
- There are many rituals and practices that Muslims use to focus on Allah

Useful Words

adhan, imam

Skills practised

- Literacy: re-wording and analysing a passage of scripture
- Analysis: reflecting on what influences young children and whether they are impacted most by nature or nurture
- Enquiry: preparing questions to ask a Muslim about his or her relationship with Allah
- Reflection: thinking about what influences them when they make decisions

Resources

- 1.4 Audio Clip: a recording of the Islamic call to prayer
- 1.4 Action Worksheet: students complete a structured spider diagram to summarize the ideas presented in the unit
- 1.4 Action Interactive Activity: students complete sentences about how Muslims put their beliefs into action
- 1.4 Lesson Player: a ready-to-go presentation with built-in resources and teacher notes
- 1 Image Gallery: a useful gallery of photos and film stills from the chapter
- 1.4 Self-Assessment Sheet: students evaluate their learning against the lesson objectives

Ideas for starters

1. Use the Starter from the *Student Book*.

2. Ask students to discuss at what age they think children can be relied upon to know right from wrong, and to take responsibility for their own spiritual lives.

3. Explain to students that one Islamic belief is that all people are born pure, but that some people then choose to live a life doing bad things. Make the statement 'no one is ever all bad' and ask students to discuss in groups what they think.

Activity guidance

Activity 3 in the *Student Book* encourages students to think about whether nature or nurture influences a person's faith the most. You might want to explain this concept to students (referring to the Islamic practice of whispering the adhan to newborn babies) before they attempt this question.

Ideas for plenaries

1. Use the Reflection from the *Student Book*. This activity encourages students to think about what has influenced them in the decisions they have made. Ask whether their parents or friends might have influenced them. Also ask them to consider the influence of their wider culture and the media. Finally, ask them to evaluate the Islamic belief that there is an inner influence from Allah.

2. Role-play a moral dilemma to get students thinking about what influences their actions. Give other students prompts to interrupt with advice at key points in the form of conscience, parents, peers, etc.

3. Follow up Activity 3 in the *Student Book* by asking several students to act out their scripts. Then ask the class to vote on whether they think nature or nurture is the most important influence.

Further class and homework activities

1. Students could learn the Useful Words and Islamic phrases from this unit for a quick test next lesson.

2. Ask students to design some graffiti, like that of graffiti artist Mohammed Ali in the *Student Book*, to express Islamic ideas about Allah.

3. 1.4 Action Worksheet on the *Islam Kerboodle*.

4. 1.4 Audio Clip on the *Islam Kerboodle*.

5. 1.4 Action Interactive Activity on the *Islam Kerboodle*.

6. Further suggestions on page 26 of this book.

The unit in brief

This unit introduces the Five Pillars of Islam, which are then expanded upon in Chapter 3. It also uses a case study example to discuss the importance of the Five Pillars to Muslims.

Key ideas

- A Muslim must perform five key duties, known as the Five Pillars (Shahadah, Salah, Zakah, Sawm, Hajj)
- Muslims believe that the Five Pillars were practised by the Prophet Muhammad, who was taught about them by the angel Jibril
- The first duty is the declaration of faith (the Shahadah)
- Saying and meaning the Shahadah for the first time is an important step for a Muslim

Skills practised

- Literacy: using key terms in another language with confidence
- Evaluation: considering which of the Five Pillars is most important and why
- Analysis: looking at what qualities might be brought out in the practice of the Five Pillars
- Reflection: thinking about whether set rules are helpful or restrictive

Resources

- 1.5 Five Pillars Film Clip: Ibrahim Yassin talks about the Five Pillars of Islam
- 1.5 Film Worksheet: students assess their understanding of the case study film clip by linking ideas to the *Student Book*
- 1.5 Five Pillars Interactive Activity: students link each of the Five Pillars with their correct definitions
- 1.5 Lesson Player: a ready-to-go presentation with built-in resources and teacher notes
- 1 Image Gallery: a useful gallery of photos and film stills from the chapter
- 1.5 Self-Assessment Sheet: students evaluate their learning against the lesson objectives

Ideas for starters

1. Use the Starter from the *Student Book*. If students think narrowly at this point, prompt them with questions about family time, personal time, etc. The idea of prioritizing is key to understanding the Five Pillars.

2. Ask students to make a Diamond 9 and rank options such as: faith, schoolwork, family time, personal time, friendships, etc. (The list of options could be drawn up by asking pairs of students to say one thing they think is important in life.)

3. Ask students, in pairs or threes, to talk about a journey they have made with a special intention. They should say what made it special and how that affected their preparations (for example, following a sports team to a special match, playing in a special concert, etc.).

Activity guidance

- Activity 3 in the *Student Book* invites students to evaluate requirements in worship. You may wish to ask students to focus specifically on the Five Pillars, but they could also think more generally about the value of duties versus being free to choose.

- You may wish to compare and contrast the Five Pillars with key teachings from other faiths, e.g. the Five Ks in Sikhism. See Unit 3.2 in the *Sikhism Student Book*.

Ideas for plenaries

1. Use the Reflection from the *Student Book*. You could ask students to feed back in pairs.

2. Ask the class to form two circles – one inside the other. Tell them to circle in opposite directions until you call stop. When you do, each student has to ask the student opposite them to define or give the Arabic word for one of the Five Pillars. You could ask other questions to check students' understanding of the key terms.

3. Ask students to come to the front one at a time and mime one of the Five Pillars, while the rest of the class try to guess which one they are miming. Award bonus points to those who can use the actual terms.

Further class and homework activities

1. As homework, ask students to use their answers to the Starter activity in the *Student Book*, or come up with their own 'five duties' based on their learning in this unit. They should then design their own diagram to represent their choices – providing annotations to explain why.

2. Show students 1.5 Five Pillars Film Clip on the *Islam Kerboodle*, and use 1.5 Film Worksheet to facilitate a discussion about the themes raised.

3. 1.5 Five Pillars Interactive Activity on the *Islam Kerboodle*.

4. Further suggestions on page 26 of this book.

Chapter 1 Further Suggestions

These suggestions are addressed directly to students.

1.1 Who are Muslims?

1 Keep a record of images from this week's media, showing – in your opinion – clothes suitable for a modern British Muslim. Make notes about each one to explain why you think the clothing is suitable. *

2 Copy and decorate the Shahadah in Arabic calligraphy. Then around it, create a visual mind-map of themes, ideas and questions from this unit. **

3 Choose one other faith and make notes about what they 'look like, do and believe'. Then write an extended paragraph that explores a key similarity or difference with Islam. Explain why this is significant, in your view. ***

1.2 Who is Allah?

1 Look at the Qur'an 50:16 in the *Student Book*. Try to write a similar description of the closeness of Allah to Muslims – but without using the 'jugular vein' idea. *

2 Obtain a list of the 99 names for Allah. Then, each day for a week, randomly choose one and produce a short reflection on it: 'What is the value of the quality? How would it impact humans? If you had this quality, how would you use it?' **

3 Do some research, and compare subhah with rosary beads in Catholicism. What are the similarities and differences? In your own opinion, are there any spiritual benefits to using objects like these? Explain your views. ***

1.3 A Whole Way of Life: Submission to Allah

1 Watch footage of Mo Farah after his Olympic win in London. What specific Islamic characteristics did he show? *

2 Organize a group of friends (about five or six) to spend a whole day following all the school rules, e.g. perfect uniform, no gum, moving quietly in the corridors, hands up, listening, etc. Present your reflections to the class. How hard was it? Did you know all the rules? Did anyone notice you behaving differently? **

3 Similarly, follow all the rules and do everything you're told at home for a day, without telling your parents your intentions. Did they notice? How can you link your experience of following rules at home to a Muslim living life as submission to Allah? ***

1.4 How do Muslims put their Beliefs into Action from Birth?

1 What words or advice would you whisper in a baby's ear, if any? Write down your thoughts and explain your reasons. **

2 Complete a detailed research task about why Muslims like calligraphy. Consider their beliefs on the matter and present examples. Then provide your own evaluation of this form of expression. You might want to refer to modern examples, like the graffiti artist Mohammed Ali (www.aerosolarabic.com). ***

3 In groups, come up with three reasons for, and three reasons against, outward expressions of faith. Choose the most convincing reason and present your case to the class – and be ready to answer questions. ***

1.5 What are the Five Pillars?

1 Choose one of the five most important things you do in your life that you suggested in response to the *Student Book* Starter. What would you need to do to make it even better this week? Write a post as if for a social networking site explaining your choice and what you will do. *

2 Imagine that you are Ibrahim from the *Student Book* case study. Write a short diary entry about the day he first said Shahadah and meant it. Try to imagine what it would have felt like. **

3 Using the statement from Activity 3 in the *Student Book* as a title, produce a detailed plan for an extended piece of writing (3–4 paragraphs). What evidence and information would you need to find out in order to argue persuasively? In your plan, write down what you would do and who you would talk to if you could. ***

Chapter 1 Assessment

Assessment in the *Student Book*

You will find an assessment task at the end of every chapter which focuses on AT2. In this chapter, the task asks students in groups to prepare for a debate on the statement: 'Belief in Allah is all a Muslim needs.'

In the *Student Book* (and on the supporting worksheets), you'll find guidance about levels of assessment that you can use to help your students understand what their work should include. You could ask them to use these criteria for self- or peer-assessment once they've completed the task.

Assessment Task for Chapter 1 (pages **18–19** of the *Islam Student Book*)

Objectives
- Demonstrate knowledge of key aspects of Islamic belief in Allah
- Show understanding of the relationship between Allah and Muslims, and how this relationship is strengthened by practice
- Reflect on your own opinions about young children following rituals

Task
Draw on your learning about Muslims' relationship with Allah to debate the statement: 'Belief in Allah is all a Muslim needs.' Do you agree or disagree? Explain your reasons.

a Prepare: In groups of four or five, identify and prepare evidence that supports each side of the argument.

b Debate: Use your prepared ideas to support what you say in a class debate about the above statement.

Assessment in *Kerboodle*

On the *Islam Kerboodle*, you'll find resources to use when introducing the assessment task to the class.

You can use the *Chapter 1 Assessment Task Presentation* as a front-of-class tool to help your students unpack the assessment criteria, and understand what is expected of them.

Chapter 1 Assessment Worksheets accompany the task, so that once you finish the presentation, your students can easily get started.

Auto-marked tests

The *Islam Kerboodle* also contains auto-marked tests for each chapter to help save you time setting questions and marking for AT1.
The test for this chapter contains 15 questions and will take most students about half an hour. Test results are automatically stored in the markbook.

Digital markbook

A markbook and a reporting function complete the *Kerboodle* assessment package, so you can keep all your students' test results and assessment scores in one place. This can include the auto-marked tests as well as pieces of work you or the students have marked by hand.

▲ Assessment resources for Chapter 1 on the *Islam Kerboodle*

Chapter 2 Overview
Where do Islamic Beliefs Come From?

Helping you deliver Key Stage 3 RE

This chapter addresses the following areas of the Programme of Study:

Key concepts

Beliefs, teachings and sources
- Interpreting teachings, sources, authorities (including the Qur'an) and ways of life in order to understand religions and beliefs

Practices and ways of life
- Understanding that religious practices are diverse, change over time, and are influenced by cultures

Key processes

Learning about religion
- Investigate the impact of religious beliefs and teachings on individuals, communities and societies, the reasons for commitment and the causes of diversity
- Explain religious beliefs, practices and commitments, including their transmission by people, texts and traditions
- Interpret a range of sources, texts, authorities, and forms of religious and spiritual expression from a variety of contexts

Learning from religion
- Express insights into the significance and value of religion for human relationships personally, locally and globally
- Express their own beliefs and ideas (including students' own attitude to authority and decision-making), using a variety of forms of expression, including creative forms and reasoned arguments

The big picture

These are the key ideas behind this chapter:

- The Qur'an is the Islamic holy book, which many Muslims read regularly. Reading in Arabic is said to bring spiritual feelings and connection with Allah.
- The Qur'an was revealed to the Prophet Muhammad over many years, and Muslims believe that it's important to know the context of passages from the Qur'an to fully understand them.
- The Qur'an is used as the central guide to behaviour for Muslims, together with the way in which the

Prophet Muhammad interpreted it in living his life. Whatever the sources of authority say, Muslims are taught to live by the law of the country in which they live.

- Muhammad was the last in a long line of Prophets, including Nuh (Noah), Ibrahim (Abraham) and Musa (Moses).
- During The Night Journey, Allah showed Muhammad how his mission was related to the Prophets who came before him and reminded him of Allah's presence.
- Both the local community and the worldwide Islamic community are very important to Muslims.

Chapter outline

Use this to give students a mental road map of the chapter:

2.1 And that's Final! The Qur'an – introduces the Islamic belief in the Qur'an as the final Word of Allah, revealed to the Prophet Muhammad

2.2 Why Me? The Prophet Muhammad – explores Muhammad's early life and the revelation of the Qur'an to him as the last in a long line of Prophets

2.3 Yes, You Can! The Story of The Night Journey – explores, using a community of enquiry, a significant time when Muhammad was taken to the heavens into the presence of Allah

2.4 Rules, Rules! How do Muslims Know How to Live? – considers different sources of authority for Muslims, and how individuals decide right from wrong and how to live their lives

2.5 Why do We Never Feel Alone? Muslims in Community – introduces the concept of the ummah and relationships between Muslims, who regard each other as a global family or community

Opportunities for assessment

Summative assessments on the *Islam Kerboodle* include auto-marked tests, interactive activities and self-assessment worksheets.

The end-of-chapter assessment task in the *Student Book* provides formative assessment. Supporting materials for the assessment task can be found on the *Islam Kerboodle*, such as the Assessment Task Presentation and the related worksheets.

There are other opportunities for assessment too. For example, you could use some of the activities or reflection points throughout each *Student Book* unit, or some of the 'Further Suggestions' at the end of this chapter.

Getting ready for this chapter

- If there is a Qur'an in school, make it available. Ideally it will have Arabic alongside an English translation. You may wish to demonstrate the respect that Muslims give to the Qur'an by keeping it on a shelf, not leaving it open when not being read, etc.

- You may wish to look up an online Qur'an (such as Qur'an.com), which will show how various translations differ slightly.

- You could provide copies of the story of The Night Journey (see Unit 2.3) ready for the lesson involving a community of enquiry.

- If you have the *Islam Kerboodle*, watch the case study film clips in advance, so that you can prepare and guide students before and during their viewing.

Objectives and outcomes for this chapter

Objectives	Unit	Outcomes
Most students will:		Most students will be able to:
• examine the Islamic belief that the Qur'an was revealed to the Prophet Muhammad • explain why and how Muslims try to live by the Qur'an • reflect on what their most trusted source of advice is.	2.1	• state when and where the Qur'an was revealed • explain why it is believed to be the Word of Allah • explain where they turn for good advice and why.
• analyse what it means to be a prophet • analyse the Islamic belief that Muhammad is the final Prophet of Islam • reflect on what it is that makes a person trustworthy.	2.2	• describe what a prophet is • place Muhammad in a timeline of Prophets from Adam onwards, including key figures like Nuh (Noah), Ibrahim (Abraham) and Musa (Moses) • reflect on how they would feel if they were entrusted with a big responsibility.
• examine the ups and downs of Muhammad's life • explore the story of The Night Journey, and respond to it philosophically • consider what helps people during difficult times.	2.3	• describe the challenges of Muhammad's early life • outline and analyse the story of Muhammad's Night Journey • describe what inspires, motivates and supports them in difficult times.
• examine the ways Muslims decide on the right way to live • explore and evaluate the main sources of guidance for Muslims • reflect on the different things that influence them.	2.4	• talk through the relational diagram from the *Student Book* • give an example of a clear Qur'anic law which must be kept no matter where someone lives, and a guideline which cannot be kept in Britain • evaluate the importance of rules.
• develop an understanding about why and how Muslims believe they are connected to all other Muslims • explore and explain the concept of jama'ah and ummah • reflect upon school as a community.	2.5	• describe the Prophet Muhammad's migration to al-Madinah and the start of the Islamic community • explain the difference between jama'ah and ummah, and why the ummah is important • analyse the concept of their school as a community.

The unit in brief

This unit introduces the Qur'an and how it was revealed to the Prophet Muhammad. It introduces the Islamic belief that the Qur'an is the final Word of Allah. Case study family members talk about how they include the Qur'an in their daily lives.

Key ideas

- The Qur'an is the Islamic holy book, and many Muslims read it regularly
- The Qur'an was revealed to the Prophet Muhammad by Allah, and is considered to be His final Word
- The Qur'an is used by Muslims as the central guide for their behaviour

Useful Words

gospels, revelation

Skills practised

- Literacy: reading and interpreting quotations
- Thinking: asking relevant questions to gain deeper understanding
- Synthesis: pulling together different information about the Qur'an to discuss alternative viewpoints

Resources

- 2.1 Qur'an Film Clip A: Sarrah Yassin talks about when she reads the Qur'an
- 2.1 Qur'an Film Clip B: Rahaf and Saad Ahmed talk about the significance of the Qur'an for them
- 2.1 Qur'an Film Clip C: Mr Atcha explains the importance of the Qur'an
- 2.1 Film Worksheet: students assess their understanding of the case study film clips by linking ideas to the *Student Book*
- 2.1 Qur'an Interactive Activity: students select true facts about the Qur'an
- 2.1 Lesson Player: a ready-to-go presentation with built-in resources and teacher notes
- 2 Image Gallery: a useful gallery of photos and film stills from the chapter
- 2.1 Self-Assessment Sheet: students evaluate their learning against the lesson objectives

Ideas for starters

1. Use the Starter from the *Student Book*. This could form the basis of a think, pair, share activity.

2. Ask students: 'If you could have a guidebook for your life, written by just one person, who would it be and why?' As an extension, you could ask students to write some short sentences that might appear in their guidebooks.

3. Search online for someone reading out loud from the Qur'an in Arabic, or use one of the audio clips on the *Islam Kerboodle*. Ask students to close their eyes and see how they feel when they listen before commenting on their experience.

Activity guidance

- The idea of Allah revealing His 'final' Word to humanity might be a confusing one for students. This is explored further in Unit 2.2, but at this point you might want to explain that texts like the Torah and the Gospels are also regarded by Muslims as holy and from Allah, but Muslims believe that their original meaning has been changed over time. The Qur'an is believed to be the final – unchanged – Word of Allah.

Ideas for plenaries

1. Use the Reflection from the *Student Book*.

2. Start off a sentence string which students have to repeat and add to as you go round the room, for example:
   - The Qur'an is used by Muslims for …

3. Ask students to say one thing that surprised them about the Qur'an, or was new to them.

Further class and homework activities

1. Give more able students the following quotation and ask: 'Why do you think Muhammad said this? What impact would it have on a Muslim?'
   'The best of those amongst you is the one who learns the Qur'an and then teaches it to others.'
   Hadith 1817

3. 2.1 Film Worksheet and 2.1 Qur'an Film Clips A–C on the *Islam Kerboodle*.

4. 2.1 Qur'an Interactive Activity on the *Islam Kerboodle*.

5. Further suggestions on page 40 of this book.

The unit in brief

This unit considers what a prophet is, as well as the Islamic idea that Muhammad was the last in a long line of prophets. Muhammad's early life is explored, and it's made clear that he is the role model for Muslims.

Key ideas

- Muslims believe that prophets are messengers sent by Allah
- The Abrahamic faiths (Christianity, Judaism, Islam) share some key figures in their history
- Muslims believe that people didn't listen properly to the earlier prophets, so Allah revealed the Qur'an to Muhammad as the last and final prophet
- Muhammad is a role model for Muslims in the way he lived his life

Useful Words

Abrahamic faiths, idol worship, polytheism

Skills practised

- Literacy: analysing a key scriptural passage
- Analysis: examining why Muhammad is considered to be the last prophet
- Reflection: imagining how it would feel to be given Muhammad's responsibility

Resources

- 2.2 Audio Clip: a reading from the Qur'an 93:1–11 in English and Arabic
- 2.2 Muhammad Timeline Worksheet: a sorting activity about the life of Muhammad
- 2.2 Prophet Interactive Activity: students link key terms related to Prophets to their correct explanations
- 2.2 Lesson Player: a ready-to-go presentation with built-in resources and teacher notes
- 2 Image Gallery: a useful gallery of photos and film stills from the chapter
- 2.2 Self-Assessment Sheet: students evaluate their learning against the lesson objectives

Ideas for starters

1. Use the Starter from the *Student Book* and discuss the importance of being trustworthy.

2. Ask the class to imagine that they have to choose someone to speak on their behalf, e.g. as a school council rep. Ask what qualities they would look for in that person.

Activity guidance

- You might want to explore the connection between the Abrahamic faiths in more detail, especially with more able students. However, you may need to explain to students that, while the three key figures mentioned in the *Student Book* are common to the three faiths, some of the stories – and the outcomes of those stories – are very different. For the Jewish stories of Abraham and Noah, see Units 1.2 and 1.3 in the *Judaism Student Book*.

- For Activity 2 in the *Student Book*, you may want to have a recording device ready, in case some students choose to record their responses.

Ideas for plenaries

1. Use the Reflection from the *Student Book*.

2. Ask students to write a short profile of Muhammad, to brief a journalist who is preparing a TV programme about Islam. Tell them that they should include what they think the most important and interesting information would be.

3. Ask students, in turn, to say how an individual event in Muhammad's life might have influenced his character.

Further class and homework activities

1. As a homework activity, ask students to research the story of Abraham, particularly the sacrifice of his son. Ask them to find out whether there are any differences between how Muslims view this story and how other faiths do. Finally, ask them to use their findings to create a colourful 'Abraham' mind-map.

2. 2.2 Muhammad Timeline Worksheet on the *Islam Kerboodle*.

3. 2.2 Prophet Interactive Activity on the *Islam Kerboodle*.

4. Further suggestions on page 40 of this book.

The unit in brief

This unit looks at the support given by Allah to the Prophet Muhammad – focusing on the story of The Night Journey. Students can reflect on the story philosophically in a community of enquiry.

Key ideas

- Allah sent support to the Prophet Muhammad and Muslims take comfort from this
- Allah showed Muhammad how his mission was related to the Prophets who came before him, and reminded him of His presence
- The Night Journey represents a spiritual journey

Useful Words

persecution, Quraysh, The Night Journey

Skills practised

- Literacy: analysing The Night Journey story
- Enquiry: considering key philosophical ideas and asking questions about The Night Journey
- Thinking: considering the definition of 'spiritual journey' and how this might relate to The Night Journey

Resources

- ⩗ 2.3 Audio Clip: a recording of The Night Journey story in the *Student Book*
- 📄 2.3 Emotions Worksheet: students evaluate events in Muhammad's life from an emotional perspective
- 🖱 2.3 Night Journey Interactive Activity: students drag the events of The Night Journey into the correct order
- 🏠 2.3 Lesson Player: a ready-to-go presentation with built-in resources and teacher notes
- 🖥 2 Image Gallery: a useful gallery of photos and film stills from the chapter
- 📄 2.3 Self-Assessment Sheet: students evaluate their learning against the lesson objectives

Ideas for starters

1. Use the Starter from the *Student Book*.

2. Discuss the Muhammad Ali quotation from the *Student Book*. Ask: 'What kinds of blows in life might defeat us? How would a person recover from them? Do you think a person ever has a right to give up?'

3. Ask students to think, pair, share the following questions: 'How important are dreams? Do you think they ever mean anything?'

Activity guidance

- The activities in this unit provide an ideal opportunity to conduct a 'community of enquiry'. In Activity 1, students choose a philosophical question to engage with in the light of The Night Journey. You may wish to generate original questions for this activity by asking students to come up with their own. Groups could complete discussions and then sit as a panel to present to – and be questioned by – the other groups. The feedback from the class could be used to enrich the work of each group.

- The activities in the unit invite students to imagine themselves into the story of The Night Journey, but you may also wish to ask students to critically examine the claim that it was a 'miracle' and really happened.

Ideas for plenaries

1. Use the Reflection from the *Student Book*.

2. Complete a class vote – firstly from the perspective of a Muslim, and then to find out students' personal opinions. The Night Journey:
    a) was a miracle
    b) was a dream
    c) supported Muhammad, so it doesn't matter what it was
    d) was a good story, but didn't really happen.

3. Ask each student to consider what they have learned in the lesson, and to write one question that they would have liked to have asked Muhammad immediately after The Night Journey ended.

4. Ask students to vote on which of the following was the most important for Muhammad (by moving around the room to form groups):
    a) Seeing paradise and hell.
    b) Speaking to earlier Prophets.
    c) Learning the right number of prayers.
    d) Approaching Allah's throne.
    e) Finding it was over in a flash.
    The different groups then have to explain their decisions.

Further class and homework activities

1. Before they open their *Student Books*, show students the photograph of Muhammad Ali from 2 Image Gallery on the *Islam Kerboodle*. Ask: 'Who is this? What do you think his life philosophy might be?' Use their responses to lead into the Starter activity in the *Student Book*.

2. Ask students to look at each event of The Night Journey and consider how it might influence a modern Muslim and strengthen their faith in Allah.

3. 2.3 Emotions Worksheet on the *Islam Kerboodle*.

4. 2.3 Night Journey Interactive Activity on the *Islam Kerboodle*.

5. Further suggestions on page 40 of this book.

The unit in brief

This unit considers different sources of authority for Muslims and how they help individuals to make decisions about right and wrong. It looks at the relationship between the Qur'an, the life of the Prophet and scholarly opinion.

Key ideas

- The Qur'an is the most important source of authority for Muslims, because it tells them how Allah wants them to live
- The ways in which the Prophet Muhammad interpreted the Qur'an help Muslims to interpret it in their daily lives
- Scholars established Shari'ah law, which is based on the Qur'an and the life of Muhammad
- Muslims live by the law of the country they live in

Useful Words

Hadith, Shari'ah, Sunnah

Skills practised

- Literacy: looking at a quotation and evaluating its relevance
- Evaluation: considering books and people as sources of authority
- Writing: writing a script for a radio conversation on the topic of adhan
- Reflection: considering and evaluating sources of guidance in their own lives

Resources

- 2.4 Audio Clip: a recording of the Ten Commandments from the Bible
- 2.4 Authority Worksheet: students complete a table to evaluate sources of authority for Muslims
- 2.4 Authority Interactive Activity: students link each source of authority to its explanation
- 2.4 Lesson Player: a ready-to-go presentation with built-in resources and teacher notes
- 2 Image Gallery: a useful gallery of photos and film stills from the chapter
- 2.4 Self-Assessment Sheet: students evaluate their learning against the lesson objectives

Ideas for starters

1. Use the Starter from the *Student Book*. Students will most likely mention people, so you could prompt them to also think about books or online sources that would be useful. You could ask them how they might use all three in making a decision.

2. Divide the class into groups and ask each student to write on a slip of paper two or three sentences from someone seeking advice about a particular issue (alternatively, you could provide a range of options). Place the slips into a bowl and ask students to take turns picking one. They then have to consider what different avenues of guidance there might be for that person.

3. Ask students to think about any recipes they may have used – in school or out. Ask them: 'Was it straightforward? Did you need help from someone to understand what it wanted you to do? Who wrote it?' You could use this discussion to introduce the issue of the reliability of texts, and how easy/difficult it can be to interpret them.

Activity guidance

- Activity 3 in the *Student Book* could be done as a role-play, rather than a written exercise. You may wish to clarify with students that the purpose of the activity is for them to consider the issue from a Muslim's perspective, and to think about what they can do to both observe British law and express their faith.

Ideas for plenaries

1. Use the Reflection from the *Student Book*. You could create a 'human continuum', by lining students up with 'always follow' at one end and 'usually rebel' at the other. You could ask individuals for their reasons.

2. Play 'Qur'an Blockbusters'. Firstly, prepare a grid of hexagons containing a letter each within a frame on the board (aim for five hexagons wide). Then split the class into two teams. Prepare questions like:

   - Name a Q that is the name of the holy book. (Qur'an)
   - Name a Ra that is a month when Muslims use the Qur'an a lot. (Ramadan), etc.

   The two teams have to take turns asking each other questions and colouring in the hexagons with their team colours. The first team across the board wins.

Further class and homework activities

- 2.4 Audio Clip could be played to students before they attempt Activity 1 in the *Student Book*.

- 2.4 Authority Worksheet on the *Islam Kerboodle*.

- 2.4 Authority Interactive Activity on the *Islam Kerboodle*.

- Further suggestions on page 40 of this book.

The unit in brief

This unit covers the concept of the ummah and relationships between Muslims. It explains why Muslims make an effort to be involved, not only with their local community, but also with other Muslims around the world.

Key ideas

- The early Islamic community was formed after Muhammad and his followers migrated to al-Madinah, after persecution in Makkah
- There are bonds of brotherhood and sisterhood between Muslims
- The modern Islamic community is both local and worldwide
- As well as being a place of worship, the mosque is also a community centre

Useful Words

jama'ah, khutbah, ummah

Skills practised

- Literacy: writing a brief for a mosque architect
- Empathy: understanding the situation of the early Muslims
- Reflection: analysing the school community and what would improve it

Resources

- 2.5 Community Worksheet: students complete a structured spider diagram about community in Islam
- 2.5 Mosque Interactive Activity: students select facilities in a mosque from a list
- 2.5 Lesson Player: a ready-to-go presentation with built-in resources and teacher notes
- 2 Image Gallery: a useful gallery of photos and film stills from the chapter
- 2.5 Self-Assessment Sheet: students evaluate their learning against the lesson objectives

Ideas for starters

1. Use the Starter from the *Student Book*. The phrase may need to be explained, if it's not one familiar to students. It means that the bonds of those related by blood are stronger than any other relationships, such as marriage or friendship. Asking whether students agree with this or not could then lead into a discussion about why Muslims call non-blood relationships 'brother' and 'sister'.

2. Ask students to draw concentric circles in their books, with themselves in the centre, and then to place other people on the outer circles. Ask why they put certain people in certain places, e.g. did they always place family members on the inner circles? This helps students to assess their attitude towards others.

Activity guidance

- It is important to get a sense of how Muhammad was regarded at the time of the revelation, and how those who stuck by him might have been treated. Perhaps this hardship made them bond together more closely. Some of them would have been cast out by their blood relatives and needed the support of others.

- For Activity 2 in the *Student Book*, some students might like to make a model of the mosque instead. Encourage them to include the correct features.

Ideas for plenaries

1. Use the Reflection from the *Student Book*. You could ask students to rank their ideas and, if possible, make recommendations to the Student Council.

2. Ask students to discuss street language like: blud, fam, bro, cuz, homie, brotha, and identify what impression these words seek to give.

Further class and homework activities

1. Ask students to look again at the story of how the Qur'an was revealed to the Prophet Muhammad, and also the treatment of the first Muslims. Ask them how they think the two may be linked.

2. 2.5 Community Worksheet on the *Islam Kerboodle*.

3. 2.5 Mosque Interactive Activity on the *Islam Kerboodle*.

4. Further suggestions on page 40 of this book.

Chapter 2 Further Suggestions

These suggestions are addressed directly to students.

2.1 And that's Final! The Qur'an

1   Choose your favourite passage from a book and read it to your classmates. Say why you like it and how it transports you to another place. *

2   Make a list of the major world events of the last few decades. Are there any relevant passages from the Qur'an that might provide Muslims with advice about any of those events? Choose an issue/event and conduct some research to find out what the Qur'an says that could be applied to that issue. **

3   Research 'The Qur'an Project', which gives copies of the Qur'an to people in the street. In pairs, debate your response to this, using your learning from the unit. Do you think the Qur'an is relevant to non-Muslims? Can it have anything to say in modern times? ***

2.2 Why Me? The Prophet Muhammad

1   Find out why Muslims do not draw pictures, or accept images, of Muhammad. Is there anything that you feel this strongly about? If so, what? Write your response as if for a social networking post. *

2   If you had to choose one person to be your 'prophet' (who you listen to and follow the advice of), who would it be? Give reasons for your choice – demonstrating that you understand what a prophet is, and referring to some of the ideas in this unit. **

3   Choose one of the people that Islam, Judaism and Christianity have in common (for instance Adam, Moses, Jesus). Are they presented as exactly the same in each faith? Write the name of the person in the centre of a piece of paper, and surround it with stories, observations and questions. ***

2.3 Yes, You Can! The Story of The Night Journey

1   Create an artwork of The Night Journey, including as many elements of the story as possible – without drawing people. Try to emphasize the aspects that you think are the most important. *

2   Imagine you are Muhammad and are being taken on The Night Journey. Write a diary or blog entry that describes what you see and how you feel. **

3   Imagine that you could write a letter to the people who laid thorns at the feet of Muhammad in the early days, or one of his other persecutors. What would you say to them now, bearing in mind how much Islam has grown and changed? **

4   If Muhammad was a Prophet, why did he need to be spiritually supported by Allah? Think of several different interesting reasons, and then write a short newspaper column debating the issue. ***

2.4 Rules, Rules! How do Muslims Know How to Live?

1   Conduct a class survey. Write students' initials on a continuum line running from 'Makes decisions instinctively', to 'Gathers lots of advice before making decisions'. Choose two of the students to interview in more detail. How do their views compare to the Islamic perspective? *

2   Watch the news or read this week's newspapers to gather examples of stories containing problems or issues. Choose one and ask yourself: 'How would a Muslim decide what to do here?' Try to find and evaluate relevant advice from Islamic sources. **

3   'Preventing the adhan in Britain is at odds with our claim that we're a multicultural society.' Do you agree with this statement? Give reasons for your answer, showing that you have thought about both points of view. ***

2.5 Why do We Never Feel Alone? Muslims in Community

1   What is a mosque? Make a flier that explains what it is for young people who want to know more. Make sure it appeals to a modern audience. *

2   'Muslims should be encouraged to spend time with people outside their own community.' Debate this statement in groups. **

3   Compare the idea of the Islamic community with that of another faith (e.g. 'the people of Israel', or 'the body of Christ'). What are the similarities and differences between them? ***

Chapter 2 Assessment

Assessment in the *Student Book*

You will find an assessment task at the end of every chapter which focuses on AT2. In this chapter, the task asks students to produce a piece of artwork depicting The Night Journey, including the key concepts and ideas it raises.

In the *Student Book* (and on the supporting worksheets), you'll find guidance about levels of assessment that you can use to help your students understand what their work should include. You could ask them to use these criteria for self- or peer-assessment once they've completed the task.

Assessment Task for Chapter 2 (pages **30–31** of the *Islam Student Book*)

Objectives

*   Investigate and analyse the key ideas that arise from the story of The Night Journey
*   Show that you understand that for Muslims, everything leads back to the Qur'an, because they consider it to be the Word of Allah
*   Express your views about the significance of The Night Journey being either real or a dream

Task

Produce a piece of artwork, or a storyboard, to show The Night Journey. See how many ideas you can get into your work.

a Prepare: Reread the section about The Night Journey in Unit 2.3, and list the key ideas.

b Produce: Create your artwork. **Remember:** Muslims do not draw pictures of the Prophet Muhammad or other people, especially not Allah.

c Evaluate: Create a display of pictures. The whole class should then use a checklist of ideas to evaluate all of the pictures.

Assessment in *Kerboodle*

On the *Islam Kerboodle*, you'll find resources to use when introducing the assessment task to the class.

You can use the *Chapter 2 Assessment Task Presentation* as a front-of-class tool to help your students unpack the assessment criteria, and understand what is expected of them.

Chapter 2 Assessment Worksheets accompany the task, so that once you finish the presentation, your students can easily get started.

▲ Assessment resources for Chapter 2 on the *Islam Kerboodle*

Auto-marked tests

The *Islam Kerboodle* also contains auto-marked tests for each chapter to help save you time setting questions and marking for AT1. The test for this chapter contains 15 questions and will take most students about half an hour. Test results are automatically stored in the markbook.

Digital markbook

A markbook and a reporting function complete the *Kerboodle* assessment package, so you can keep all your students' test results and assessment scores in one place. This can include the auto-marked tests as well as pieces of work you or the students have marked by hand.

Chapter 3 Overview
Belonging to the Islamic Faith

Helping you deliver Key Stage 3 RE

This chapter addresses the following areas of the Programme of Study:

Key concepts

Practices and ways of life
- Exploring the impact of religions and beliefs on how people live their lives

Expressing meaning
- Appreciating that individuals and cultures express their beliefs and values through many different forms

Identity, diversity and belonging
- Understanding how individuals develop a sense of identity and belonging through faith or belief

Key processes

Learning about religion
- Investigate the impact of religious beliefs and teachings on individuals, communities and societies, the reasons for commitment and the causes of diversity

Learning from religion
- Evaluate beliefs, commitments and the impact of religion in the contemporary world
- Express insight into the significance and value of religion for human relationships personally, locally and globally

The big picture

These are the key ideas behind this chapter:

- Each of the Five Pillars challenges Muslims to demonstrate their love for Allah in a different way, which develops the Islamic character, e.g. submission, responsibility, patience, discipline, self-control, commitment.

- Muslims can choose whether or not to wear Islamic dress. There are also many cultural influences on dress. Some people stereotype Muslims because of their clothing, even though much of it is more cultural than Islamic.

- Festivals are a time for families and friends to have fun, but the main Eid festivals are linked to religious history and have special meaning.

Chapter outline

Use this to give students a mental road map of the chapter:

3.1 Why do Muslims Pray Each Day? – explains why Muslims pray so often and what it involves

3.2 Looking After Brothers and Sisters: Zakah and Sadaqah – explains zakah and sadaqah and the differences between them

3.3 Why is Self-restraint Important? Fasting in Ramadan – introduces fasting and explains that the emphasis is on the development of patience and self-restraint, not just on not eating

3.4 Would you go the Distance? The Pilgrimage of Hajj – explains the Hajj pilgrimage and rituals, and also why Hajj is important from a historical perspective

3.5 Are You What You Eat? Halal and Haram Food – discusses Islamic food rules, including alcohol and attitudes to certain foods

3.6 What do You See When You Look at Me? Islamic Dress – explains Islamic dress guidelines and the requirement to dress modestly, as well as the influence of culture

3.7 How Important is Remembering the Past? Eid Festivals – describes the two Eid festivals and why they are celebrated

Opportunities for assessment

Summative assessments on the *Islam Kerboodle* include auto-marked tests, interactive activities, and self-assessment worksheets.

The end-of-chapter assessment task in the *Student Book* provides formative assessment. Supporting materials for the assessment task can be found on the *Islam Kerboodle*, such as the Assessment Task Presentation and the related worksheets.

There are other opportunities for assessment too. For example, you could use some of the activities or reflection points throughout each *Student Book* unit, or some of the 'Further Suggestions' at the end of this chapter.

Getting ready for this chapter

- Find out the dates of Ramadan and Hajj this year. There are some useful festival guides on www.bbc.co.uk/religion.

- For Unit 3.5, you might like to obtain equipment to turn the fridge magnet designs into real fridge magnets.
- If the school has a cross-curricular focus, organize for the Food Technology Department to be involved during the teaching of Unit 3.5.

- Collect fashion and other magazines with images of women, so that students can decide which are modest and compare them with Islamic dress requirements during Unit 3.6.
- If you have the *Islam Kerboodle*, watch the case study film clips in advance, so that you can prepare and guide students before and during their viewing.

Objectives and outcomes for this chapter

Objectives	Unit	Outcomes
Most students will:		Most students will be able to:
• develop an understanding about why Muslims have set times for prayer • analyse and explain the significance of prayer in Muslims' lives • reflect on how they please people they care about.	3.1	• explain why Muslims pray five times a day at set times • link prayer to submission and also to thanksgiving • think about what they give up time for.
• investigate why Muslims believe that giving to charity is essential • explain the difference between zakah and sadaqah • reflect on whether giving time is more important than giving money.	3.2	• describe zakah and its importance to Muslims • explain the difference between compulsory and voluntary giving • give a reasoned opinion about the merits of financial giving.
• develop an understanding about why Muslims fast in Ramadan • evaluate the Islamic view that self-restraint is a valuable skill • reflect on their own views about how difficult it is to deny ourselves the things we want.	3.3	• define Ramadan and outline the fasting requirements • give their opinion on the reasons for fasting • outline a time when they found it hard to be patient.
• explore Hajj as an example of Islamic pilgrimage • identify the features which make Hajj spiritual • reflect on times when they consider the meaning of life.	3.4	• describe what happens on Hajj • explain why Hajj is different from tourism • write an account of a journey that is comparable to pilgrimage.
• explain reasons for Islamic food rules • develop an understanding of halal and haram • consider the relevance of food rules in modern times.	3.5	• list at least three Islamic food rules • say what they think 'pure' might mean in the context of food • describe the role of food in their lives.
• develop an understanding about and explain why some Muslims dress the way they do • analyse what affects the way people dress • reflect on and discuss whether it matters how we dress.	3.6	• describe requirements of Islamic dress • describe different interpretations of Islamic dress • give their response to stereotyping people by their clothing.
• examine how and why Muslims celebrate two main Eid festivals • identify key Islamic beliefs shown by the story of Eid-ul-Adha • evaluate and explain reasons for remembering historical events.	3.7	• describe the two main Eid festivals in Islam and explain what each involves and why • explain the relevance of Abraham's sacrifice and Qurbani for Muslims • compare Eid celebrations with their own experiences.

The unit in brief

This unit outlines why many Muslims pray five times each day. It covers the fact that the Prophet Muhammad was told how many times to pray, and that there are instructions in holy texts. It then moves on to what objects Muslims use to help them to pray, and what kinds of words they might say.

Key ideas

- Prayer is about following Allah's wishes and expressing worship to Him
- Prayer is one of the Five Pillars (salah)
- There is a difference between set prayer (salah) and personal prayer (du'a)

Useful Words

du'a, Makkah, salah

Skills practised

- Critical thinking: considering the advantages and disadvantages of repeating the same words when praying
- Evaluation: expressing thoughts about prayer aids
- Analysis: exploring the reasons why there are two different kinds of prayer

Resources

- 3.1 Audio Clip: a recording of an Islamic prayer in English and Arabic
- 3.1 Prayer Film Clip: the Yassin family during their prayer time
- 3.1 Prayer Worksheet: students complete a structured piece of writing on the topic of prayer
- 3.1 Prayer Interactive Activity: students link key words to do with prayer with their correct explanation
- 3.1 Lesson Player: a ready-to-go presentation with built-in resources and teacher notes
- 3 Image Gallery: a useful gallery of photos and film stills from the chapter
- 3.1 Self-Assessment Sheet: students evaluate their learning against the lesson objectives

Ideas for starters

1. Use the Starter from the *Student Book*.

2. Ask students whether they have set times for doing homework and any other responsibilities, and whether they think it's better to have a timetable for this — or to do it when they feel like it. Aim to draw out the advantages and disadvantages.

3. Play word association. Ask students, in 60 seconds, to list all the words they can think of in response to the words 'Islamic prayer'.

Activity guidance

- You may wish to draw out the idea of prayer being a ritual. Many Muslims would say that whilst prayer is a duty, they regard it as a privilege to have time put aside to pray to Allah. To compare with other faiths, see Unit 3.4 in the *Christianity Student Book* and Unit 3.2 in the *Hinduism Student Book*.

- Activity 2 should allow students the opportunity to express their own views about prayer, e.g. those who do not believe in a god should be encouraged to express this. Students should be encouraged to highlight specific aspects of Islamic prayer that they like or dislike and why.

Ideas for plenaries

1. Use the Reflection from the *Student Book*.

2. Ask students to line up and create a human continuum, according to how much they agree or disagree with various statements, such as:
   - It's a good idea for Muslims to have set times to pray.
   - It's a good idea for Muslims to always use the same words when they pray.
   - Prayer is pointless.

3. List the different sources related to prayer in the *Student Book* (Yassin family photo, prayer aids, quotes from scripture) and ask what students have learned from each one. This could be done in the form of group work, where each group takes a source, and sets quiz questions for the other groups.

4. Ask students to focus on a particular Islamic practice, e.g. taking care of prayer mats. Using sticky notes, or a creative display, ask students to make a class word wall about how Muslims feel about prayer, based on these particular practices.

Further class and homework activities

1. Firstly, get a prayer timetable for today from www.islamicfinder.org. Then put students into small groups (ideally ten). Pair up the groups and allocate a prayer time to each pair. The first group in the pair should role-play something that might get in the way of the prayer at that time of day. The second group should then role-play how that situation could be resolved.

2. 3.1 Prayer Worksheet on the *Islam Kerboodle*.

3. 3.1 Prayer Interactive Activity on the *Islam Kerboodle*.

4. You could show students 3.1 Prayer Film Clip or play 3.1 Audio Clip on the *Islam Kerboodle* as examples of Islamic prayer.

5. Further suggestions on page 58 of this book.

The unit in brief

This unit outlines one of the Five Pillars – zakah – as well as sadaqah, and the difference between them. It covers the collection of zakah and the ways in which it may be spent. The importance of sadaqah is outlined by quotations from holy texts. It makes clear that sadaqah need not be financial, but can be any deed done for the sake of Allah.

Key ideas

- Zakah is one of the Five Pillars of Islam
- Zakah is a percentage of a Muslim's wealth, given to the poor and needy
- Zakah sets a minimum to financial giving, but Muslims can choose to give more – and not just financially
- Sadaqah is a different type of giving, not necessarily financial, done freely and for the sake of Allah (rather than any personal interest)

Useful Words

Eid-ul-Fitr, sadaqah, zakah

Skills practised

- Numeracy: calculating zakah; considering the reasons why zakah is a percentage, rather than a fixed amount
- Literacy: reading and reflecting on passages from holy texts
- Thinking: considering reasons why there are two types of giving for Muslims
- Evaluation: considering arguments for and against a statement about whether individuals have a responsibility to take care of poor people

Resources

- 📄 3.2 Zakah Worksheet: students complete a series of written activities to reinforce the unit content
- ↖ 3.2 Zakah Interactive Activity: students drag expenses to the correct columns, depending on whether zakah can or cannot be spent on them
- 🎓 3.2 Lesson Player: a ready-to-go presentation with built-in resources and teacher notes
- 🖥 3 Image Gallery: a useful gallery of photos and film stills from the chapter
- 📄 3.2 Self-Assessment Sheet: students evaluate their learning against the lesson objectives

Ideas for starters

1. Use the Starter from the *Student Book*. Students could discuss the first part of the activity in pairs. You might have to prompt them to think not only about possessions, but also money and time. Feed back as a class and identify the things that students find easy to share – and the things they find hard. Discuss whether people have a responsibility to share.

2. Ask students whether they've ever done anything kind for someone – but without telling them they've done it. Ask them why or why not. Encourage students to think about the idea that motives for generosity can include the desire to receive gratitude.

Ideas for plenaries

1. Use the Reflection from the *Student Book*.

2. Give each student a sticky note, or small piece of paper. Ask them to write down:

   a) What percentage they would be willing to give as zakah, if they were able.

   b) One thing that they would find easy to do as sadaqah to make the school a better place.

3. Ask students to think of small acts that they could do to help the class in some way. Ask them to write them down on a piece of paper and put them anonymously in a box. Then ask each student to draw out one of the pieces of paper. Set them the challenge of completing the task without letting anyone know.

4. Debate the statement: 'No one should have to pay membership fees to join a club.'

Further class and homework activities

1. A game of 'quick fire calculations' would provide an opportunity for a cross-curricular activity with Maths. Split the class into two teams, which then have to take turns to state an amount of wealth. The other team has to calculate zakah at 2.5% in a given time. Award points if this is achieved. This activity could be varied to suit the class ability level.

2. As a homework activity, ask students to come up with arguments for and against the statement: 'Zakah creates a sense of togetherness amongst Muslims.'

3. 3.2 Zakah Worksheet on the *Islam Kerboodle*.

4. 3.2 Zakah Interactive Activity on the *Islam Kerboodle*.

5. Further suggestions on page 58 of this book.

3.3 Why is Self-restraint Important? Fasting in Ramadan

The unit in brief

This unit looks at the fourth pillar of Islam – sawm, or 'fasting'. The emphasis is on the development of patience and self-restraint (not just on not eating). Ibrahim and Sarrah Yassin from the case study families explain why they fast.

Key ideas

- Sawm is the fourth pillar of Islam, and according to the Qur'an Muslims should practise it every year during Ramadan
- Muslims believe that patience, discipline and self-restraint can be developed through abstaining from prohibited acts for an extended period
- Many Muslims also believe that fasting helps them to develop empathy with those less fortunate than themselves

Skills practised

- Literacy: reflecting on the differences between the terms fasting, starving and dieting
- Empathy: considering the idea that fasting helps people to understand the sufferings of others
- Reflection: considering self-restraint and whether it's easy to be patient

Resources

- 3.3 Ramadan Film Clip: Ibrahim and Sarrah Yassin talk about why they fast during Ramadan
- 3.3 Film Worksheet: students assess their understanding of the case study film clip by linking ideas to the *Student Book*
- 3.3 Ramadan Interactive Activity: students fill the gaps in a paragraph about Ramadan
- 3.3 Lesson Player: a ready-to-go presentation with built-in resources and teacher notes
- 3 Image Gallery: a useful gallery of photos and film stills from the chapter
- 3.3 Self-Assessment Sheet: students evaluate their learning against the lesson objectives

Ideas for starters

1. Use the Starter from the *Student Book*. Lead into a discussion about how, for most people in Britain, there is always food readily available, but ask students to consider that – even within

Britain – there might not be. Then ask them to consider what they think it would be like for a person to have to wait all day to eat when they are really hungry. Explain that, during Ramadan, British Muslims fast for up to 18 hours a day, but most know that there will be a decent meal at the end of the day. Then explain that many Muslims give to charity to make sure that less-fortunate Muslims around the world receive a meal after fasting.

2. If the class is likely to have some understanding of Lent in the Christian calendar, it might be useful to start by talking about why Christians give up something for Lent, and how some fast for one whole day at the start of Lent.

3. Ask students to list ways in which people control themselves, e.g. counting to ten, breathing deeply, etc. You could then ask what makes it hard to have self-restraint sometimes.

Activity guidance

- For Activity 1, discuss how we use words like 'starving' to indicate 'very hungry'. Dieting might involve going without food, or restricting food choices. For many Muslims, fasting involves not allowing anything to be taken into the body – not even medicines or water. You might want to clarify with students that fasting is done in obedience to Allah, as one of the Five Pillars (not to achieve a personal goal like losing weight).

- Activity 3 could be explored by asking students to act out scenarios to each other in groups for how they might develop certain qualities.

Ideas for plenaries

1. Use the Reflection from the *Student Book*. You could ask students to share their thoughts in pairs.

2. Ask students to give one way in which their self-control (or lack of it) affects others.

3. Ask students what they would find hardest to give up for Ramadan – and what would give them the strength to do it.

Further class and homework activities

1. Show students 3.3 Ramadan Film Clip on the *Islam Kerboodle*, and use 3.3 Film Worksheet to facilitate a discussion about the themes raised.

2. 3.3 Ramadan Interactive Activity on the *Islam Kerboodle*.

3. Further suggestions on page 58 of this book.

3.4 Would you Go the Distance? The Pilgrimage of Hajj

The unit in brief

This unit describes Hajj pilgrimage. Students learn about why Muslims believe pilgrimage is important, where they go, and what rituals they complete. This unit also considers why Hajj is important from a historical perspective, and some of the challenges that Muslims face, including a case study.

Key ideas

- Hajj is the fifth pillar of Islam
- A pilgrimage is a spiritual journey
- Many Muslims believe that they should complete Hajj for the sake of Allah, out of thanks for what He has given to people, but it is not always possible
- The Ka'bah is a holy, central place of worship in Makkah

Useful Words

Ka'bah, pilgrimage, Shaytan

Skills practised

- Literacy: using imaginative writing in a five-sense poem or diary entry
- Enquiry: discovering the rituals involved in pilgrimage and finding out why they are practised
- Thinking: considering what makes a pilgrimage different from a normal journey
- Synthesis: understanding how history affects the present day

Resources

- 3.4 Hajj Film Clip: Mr and Mrs Yassin talk about their experience of Hajj
- 3.4 Hajj Worksheet: students analyse a Hajj photo
- 3.4 Audio Clip: a guided meditation on 'peace'
- 3.4 Hajj Interactive Activity: students drag activities to be completed on Hajj into the correct order
- 3.4 Lesson Player: a ready-to-go presentation with built-in resources and teacher notes
- 3 Image Gallery: a useful gallery of photos and film stills from the chapter
- 3.4 Self-Assessment Sheet: students evaluate their learning against the lesson objectives

Ideas for starters

1. Use the Starter from the *Student Book*. This helps students to think about what makes a place significant, so that discussion can be had later about why Makkah is significant.

2. Ask students to talk for 60 seconds about an important journey they made (who, what, when, where, why, how). They should feed back each other's stories.

Activity guidance

- Starter questions about journeys made, like Starter 2 above, bring out the main points about travel. In order to introduce pilgrimage, encourage students to look for ideas about: key events in the history of faith, commitment/hardship, bringing merit, forgiveness, hope for miracles or healing, duty, life-changing experience and refreshing faith by showing discipline or committing themselves. You could make this a checklist and, if there is knowledge about other pilgrimage (e.g. Christian pilgrimage to Lourdes), the different reasons could be explored.

- Explain to students that non-Muslims are not allowed to go to Makkah, because it's considered by many to be too sacred to be a tourist destination. You may wish to use this information to highlight the differences between 'pilgrimage' and 'travelling'.

Ideas for plenaries

1. Use the Reflection from the *Student Book*.

2. Read out to the class: 'It is said that a journey of a thousand miles begins with one step'. Then ask students what first step they would recommend to a Muslim who wants to go on Hajj.

3. Ask students to make suggestions about what someone could do after pilgrimage to keep the feeling alive.

Further class and homework activities

1. Encourage students to reflect on 'peace' on Hajj with a guided meditation (3.4 Audio Clip on the *Islam Kerboodle* will guide them through this process).

2. Ask students to write a letter (or record a message) to someone who has been on Hajj – asking them questions about it, and giving their opinion about the relevance of pilgrimage in the modern world.

3. The British Museum ran a Hajj exhibition in 2012. You could show students some of the images and the exhibition video at www.

britishmuseum.org/hajj. Invite students to evaluate the different expressions of devotion to Hajj that they see.

4. 3.4 Hajj Film Clip on the *Islam Kerboodle*.

5. 3.4 Hajj Worksheet on the *Islam Kerboodle*.

6. 3.4 Hajj Interactive Activity on the *Islam Kerboodle*.

7. Further suggestions on page 58 of this book.

The unit in brief

This unit covers Islamic food rules, including eating, alcohol, and attitudes to food (from the perspective of a case study family).

Key ideas

- Certain instructions are given in the Qur'an about food and drink
- Some foods are deemed 'halal' (lawful), and others are deemed 'haram' (unlawful)
- Many Muslims only eat halal food and do not drink alcohol
- The Prophet Muhammad taught that Muslims should avoid greediness

Skills practised

- Thinking: considering how foods can be 'pure'
- Empathy: asking questions to consider food rules from an Islamic perspective
- Reflection: reflecting on whether students think about where their food comes from

Resources

- 3.5 Food Film Clip: Mrs Atcha explains the concept of halal food
- 3.5 Film Worksheet: students assess their understanding of the case study film clip by linking ideas to the *Student Book*
- 3.5 Halal Haram Interactive Activity: students decide whether statements should go in the 'halal' or 'haram' column
- 3.5 Lesson Player: a ready-to-go presentation with built-in resources and teacher notes
- 3 Image Gallery: a useful gallery of photos and film stills from the chapter
- 3.5 Self-Assessment Sheet: students evaluate their learning against the lesson objectives

Ideas for starters

1. Use the Starter from the *Student Book*. This allows students to consider the pleasure of eating, and the enjoyment many people get from food. This will be a useful contrast when the topic is discussed. Discussing cravings could also lead to discussion about the idea that many Muslims believe Allah gave food for sustenance, and that it is part of the 'test' not to be greedy.

2. Ask students to write down what they ate in the last 24 hours (caution is advised if there are SEN issues, in which case it might be safer to write down a typical family menu). Ask whether any of them ate things simply because someone said they should (like Brussels sprouts!).

3. Ask students what they understand by the terms 'halal' and 'haram'. This could lead to a discussion about particular foods, and also a discussion about the idea that Muslims believe that what they eat (and how it is prepared) is important.

Activity guidance

- When considering why many Muslims have food laws, you may wish to explore with students that some laws are about outcome (for example, alcohol), and others are more about obedience (for example, pork).

- You may also decide to explore the idea that physical health might be linked to spiritual or emotional health. Students could consider the Christian idea that the body is a 'temple' of the Holy Spirit. A modern idea might be that of a sports team which is physically fit but also has the right mental attitude.

Ideas for plenaries

1. Use the Reflection from the *Student Book*.

2. Ask students to write down three key pieces of advice they would give a Muslim so that they have the right attitude to food.

3. Get the class to summarize Islamic food rules by going round the room – each student giving one word and the rest following on to make a sentence.

Further class and homework activities

1. Ask students to create an advertisement showing what they would do about the problem of some people having too much food, while others have barely enough.

2. Ask students to prepare a persuasive speech that either recommends the school canteen serves halal meat, or explains why it should not.

3. 3.5 Food Film Clip and the accompanying 3.5 Film Worksheet on the *Islam Kerboodle*.

4. 3.5 Halal Haram Interactive Activity on the *Islam Kerboodle*.

5. Further suggestions on page 58 of this book.

3.6 What do You See When You Look at Me? Islamic Dress

The unit in brief

This unit discusses Islamic dress, and introduces the idea that Muslims interpret teachings in a variety of ways. The impact of factors such as culture and climate are considered. A case study family is used to introduce the idea that the choice to wear Islamic dress is one that many Muslim women make for themselves.

Key ideas

- Muslims dress differently depending on their culture, climate and beliefs
- The Qur'an requires that Muslim men and women dress modestly. It also states that the 'inner' character is more important than wearing the right clothing.
- Many Muslims believe that they have the freedom to choose whether to wear Islamic clothing or not.

Useful Words

modesty, righteousness

Skills practised

- Literacy: reading a key passage from the Qur'an and answering comprehension questions before expressing insight
- Interpretation: applying key texts to modern situations and British culture
- Synthesis and Application: designing clothing for young Muslims in Britain, bearing in mind the information given in the unit

Resources

- ⎓ 3.6 Audio Clip: a passage from the Qur'an (24:31) in English and Arabic with instructions to Muslim women
- ▦ 3.6 Hijab Film Clip: Mrs Atcha explains why she wears the hijab
- ▤ 3.6 Film Worksheet: students assess their understanding of the case study film clip by linking ideas to the *Student Book*
- ⬉ 3.6 Clothing Interactive Activity: students link key words about dress with their definitions
- ⌂ 3.6 Lesson Player: a ready-to-go presentation with built-in resources and teacher notes
- ▭ 3 Image Gallery: a useful gallery of photos and film stills from the chapter
- ▤ 3.6 Self-Assessment Sheet: students evaluate their learning against the lesson objectives

Ideas for starters

1. Use the Starter from the *Student Book*. Ask students to consider why they choose their clothes – is it just functional (e.g. to keep warm), or for style reasons? You could use these discussions to introduce the idea of religious clothing. Ask students whether they think people are 'made' to wear it, or whether they choose to.

2. Ask students to look at the artwork in this unit, alongside any other images that you provide. Some students may already have strong impressions or opinions about Islamic dress. Therefore, you could start the lesson by asking them to relay their impressions.

Activity guidance

- You may want to clarify with students when Muslim women are expected to cover themselves, according to the Qur'an, and when they do not need to. A woman is free to dress as she pleases in her own home, and in front of female friends. On other occasions and situations women may choose to cover themselves or dress modestly.

- Before getting students to undertake Activity 3 in the *Student Book*, you could engage them by showing various images of British celebrities – ranging from modest to less so.

Ideas for plenaries

1. Use the Reflection from the *Student Book*.

2. Using sticky notes, ask students to note down one thing they have learned about Islamic attitudes to dress, and one question they still have. In groups, students should share and discuss their ideas.

Further class and homework activities

1. Use 3 Image Gallery to show the artwork of Islamic dress. This could be used alongside Starter 2 above.

2. 3.6 Audio Clip on the *Islam Kerboodle* provides a longer quotation than that given in the *Student Book*. You could ask students to summarize the passage and then consider why women might be restricted in this particular way.

3. 3.6 Hijab Film Clip and the accompanying 3.6 Film Worksheet on the *Islam Kerboodle.*

4. 3.6 Clothing Interactive Activity on the *Islam Kerboodle.*

5. Further suggestions on page 58 of this book.

3.7 How Important is Remembering the Past? Eid Festivals

The unit in brief

This unit introduces the two main Eid festivals – Eid-ul-Adha and Eid-ul-Fitr. Students learn about the celebratory and spiritual aspects of these festivals, including the use of a case study.

Key ideas

- Eid-ul-Adha is associated with the Prophet Ibrahim's sacrifice
- Eid-ul-Adha reminds Muslims to develop obedience and trust, which are key to their relationship with Allah
- Eid-ul-Fitr means 'festival of breaking the fast' at the end of Ramadan
- The Eid festivals are a time for families and fun after spiritually significant periods

Skills practised

- Literacy: writing a diary entry from the point of view of a Muslim
- Thinking: considering the meaning of 'sacrifice' in this context
- Reflection: reflecting on celebrations in students' own lives

Resources

- 3.7 Eid Film Clip: Sarrah and Ibrahim Yassin talk about how they celebrate Eid

- 3.7 Film Worksheet: students assess their understanding of the case study film clip by linking ideas to the *Student Book*

- 3.7 Eid Interactive Activity: students decide whether statements should be dragged to the 'Eid-ul-Adha' or 'Eid-ul-Fitr' column

- 3.7 Lesson Player: a ready-to-go presentation with built-in resources and teacher notes

- 3 Image Gallery: a useful gallery of photos and film stills from the chapter

- 3.7 Self-Assessment Sheet: students evaluate their learning against the lesson objectives

Ideas for starters

1. Use the Starter from the *Student Book*. When thinking about different kinds of parties, students should be directed to discuss family gatherings and what happens.

2. Ask students to consider what thing they would find most difficult to give up if someone important said they should.

Activity guidance

- The exact Eid dates depend on when Hajj ends – information available from www.bbc.co.uk/religion.

- Activity 3 in the *Student Book* should encourage students to consider the difference between a non-religious party and a religious festival. They should consider the essential religious elements.

- Activity 1 could lead into a discussion about why people hold onto key stories from the past. Higher ability students may wish to discuss whether it's important that stories can be proven to be true or not. Ask whether students think that they still have significance if they simply illustrate a point.

Ideas for plenaries

1. Use the Reflection from the *Student Book*.

2. Divide the class up into pairs. One student in each pair should imagine that he or she went to an Eid party at the home of a Muslim friend. The pair should then write text messages to each other about it.

3. Ask students to list either four or nine aspects of Eid, and to rank them in a diamond to show which they think are the most important.

Further class and homework activities

1. Ask students to find out the date for Eid-ul-Adha this year. What happens in their local community at this time?

2. 3.7 Eid Film Clip and the accompanying 3.7 Film Worksheet on the *Islam Kerboodle*.

3. 3.7 Eid Interactive Activity on the *Islam Kerboodle*.

4. Further suggestions on page 58 of this book.

Chapter 3 Further Suggestions

These suggestions are addressed directly to students.

3.1 Why do Muslims Pray Each Day?

1 Research what happens during Islamic prayers and, if possible, watch someone perform salah. What are your initial impressions and questions? *

2 Obtain an Islamic prayer timetable and look at how it changes with the seasons. Ask your teacher to organize a visit to the local mosque. *

3 How would you explain prayer requirements to your family if a Muslim friend was coming for dinner? **

3.2 Looking After Brothers and Sisters: Zakah and Sadaqah

1 Write a list of the things you love so much that it would be very difficult to give them away. How would you feel if you had to? *

2 If you are interested in financial matters, find out about the National Insurance tax and then find out what the government spends your parents' contributions on. In what ways is this similar to or different from zakah? **

3 'Giving is far better than receiving.' Evaluate the truth of this statement in a format of your choice – making sure that you refer to Islamic teaching and your own opinion. Extend your response by also considering another belief system. ***

3.3 Why is Self-restraint Important? Fasting in Ramadan

1 Note down three reasons why Muslims fast at Ramadan. Discuss them with a partner and decide whether or not they would be enough to make you go without food. Is there anything you'd like to know more about? If so, what? *

2 Think about what you know about healthy eating and plan a menu for someone who is fasting so that they get the correct nutrients in their meals before dawn prayer and after sunset prayer. *

3 Imagine that you are Sarrah or Ibrahim from the case study in the *Student Book*. Write a blog post for one full day of Ramadan. You may need to carry out extra research to make sure that you refer to the various rituals they will go through. Using the information in this unit, try to express how you would feel. **/***

3.4 Would you Go the Distance? The Pilgrimage of Hajj

1 Research Sir Richard Burton, the non-Muslim explorer who entered Makkah. Storyboard his experiences. *

2 Do you think that Sir Richard Burton was right to pretend that he was a Muslim in order to enter Makkah? Write a letter to him, giving your response to his experience. **

3 Role-play or write a letter to someone who wants to go on Hajj but is unable to. What would you say to them? ***

3.5 Are You What You Eat? Halal and Haram Food

1 Should cost be a factor in deciding whether a canteen – either at school or at work – should provide halal food? Debate in class. **

2 Find out what 'freeganism' is and what it involves. Would this kind of eating be acceptable to Muslims? Role-play, or write a script for, a conversation between a Muslim and a 'Freegan' about their attitudes to food. ***

3.6 What do You See When You Look at Me? Islamic Dress

1 Research different styles of head covering for Muslim women. Are any more or less acceptable in Britain? Create a short fact file with information on each type. *

2 'Little girls should not wear the hijab, because they are not aware of the need for modesty.' How might Mrs Atcha from the *Student Book* case study respond to this? **

3 'Expecting women to cover their heads is a form of oppression.' Using the information in this unit, consider arguments for and against this view in a class debate. ***

3.7 How Important is Remembering the Past? Eid Festivals

1 In what ways is Eid-ul-Fitr different from Eid-ul-Adha? Spend two minutes sharing what you know with a partner. *

2 Imagine that you are planning an Eid-ul-Adha celebration with some British Muslim friends. What activities will you include and what food will you serve? How could you ensure that the story of the Prophet Ibrahim is remembered? **

Chapter 3 Assessment

Assessment in the *Student Book*

You will find an assessment task at the end of every chapter which focuses on AT2. In this chapter, the task asks students to draw on their learning about the Five Pillars, festivals and the Islamic community to plan an Eid party for an Islamic youth group.

In the *Student Book* (and on the supporting worksheets), you'll find guidance about levels of assessment that you can use to help your students understand what their work should include. You could ask them to use these criteria for self- or peer-assessment once they've completed the task.

Assessment Task for Chapter 3 (pages **46–47** of the *Islam Student Book*)

Objectives	Task
• Demonstrate that you know how being a Muslim affects day-to-day life and community events • Demonstrate empathy with Muslims trying to follow the rules of Islam	Draw on your learning about the Five Pillars, festivals and the Islamic community to plan an Eid party for an Islamic youth group. Be prepared to present your plan to the mosque committee for approval. **a** Prepare: In groups of three or four, decide what is important to a Muslim about Ramadan and Eid. **b** Plan: Use your research to plan all aspects of the party. Decide how you will persuade people to help you get the party ready. **c** Evaluate: Each group should vote on which of the planned parties they would prefer to attend, and explain why.

Assessment in *Kerboodle*

On the *Islam Kerboodle*, you'll find resources to use when introducing the assessment task to the class.

You can use the *Chapter 3 Assessment Task Presentation* as a front-of-class tool to help your students unpack the assessment criteria, and understand what is expected of them.

Chapter 3 Assessment Worksheets accompany the task, so that once you finish the presentation, your students can easily get started.

▲ Assessment resources for Chapter 3 on the *Islam Kerboodle*

Auto-marked tests

The *Islam Kerboodle* also contains auto-marked tests for each chapter to help save you time setting questions and marking for AT1. The test for this chapter contains 15 questions and will take most students about half an hour. Test results are automatically stored in the markbook.

Digital markbook

A markbook and a reporting function complete the *Kerboodle* assessment package, so you can keep all your students' test results and assessment scores in one place. This can include the auto-marked tests as well as pieces of work you or the students have marked by hand.

Living Faiths Assessment

Student Book
- Assessment Task
- Levels Guidance

Kerboodle
- Auto-Marked Test
- Assessment Task Presentation
- Assessment Worksheets

Helping you deliver Key Stage 3 RE

This chapter addresses the following areas of the Programme of Study:

Key concepts

Beliefs, teachings and sources
- Understanding and responding critically to beliefs and attitudes

Meaning, purpose and truth
- Exploring some of the ultimate questions that confront humanity (including life and death, suffering and creation), and responding imaginatively to them

Values and commitments
- Understanding how moral values and a sense of obligation can come from beliefs and experience.
- Evaluating their own and others' values in order to make informed, rational choices

Key processes

Learning about religion
- Evaluate how religious beliefs and teachings inform answers to ultimate questions and ethical issues
- Analyse religious beliefs, arguments and ideas

Learning from religion
- Reflect on the relationship between beliefs, teachings, world issues and ultimate questions
- Express their own beliefs and ideas, using a variety of forms of expression

The big picture

These are the key ideas behind this chapter:

- This life is a preparation for eternal life after death, which can be spent in either heaven or hell.
- Life's challenges are sent by Allah as tests to cause Muslims to struggle in the face of difficulties to behave and develop as Allah wants them to.
- The Earth is not owned by humans and cannot be used simply as they wish – they answer to Allah for their actions.
- Allah is in charge of creation and science is not necessarily in conflict with this idea.
- It's wrong to end a life, because Allah gives life and decides when people will die. However, there are

some circumstances when killing can be allowed for a 'just cause'.

Chapter outline

Use this to give students a mental road map of the chapter:

4.1 Do You Live For the Afterlife? – introduces the Islamic idea that this life is merely a preparation for eternal life

4.2 Death – the End or the Beginning? – considers Islamic attitudes to death and bereavement, looking at beliefs and rituals

4.3 Is Life a Test? The Two Types of Jihad – explains the struggles to be a good Muslim, and outlines the differences between the greater and lesser jihads

4.4 How Can We Live With Suffering? – explains that suffering is part of the test which Muslims face from Allah, and explores the idea that suffering can lead to good things

4.5 Are We Responsible? Khalifah for Muslims – considers individual responsibility for natural resources and the importance of compassion

4.6 Does it Matter How the World was Created? – explores Islamic ideas about creation and science – that Allah is in charge of creation

4.7 Is Killing Ever Justified? War and Capital Punishment – looks at issues surrounding killing in Islam, which is allowed if it's for a 'just cause'

Opportunities for assessment

Summative assessments on the *Islam Kerboodle* include auto-marked tests, interactive activities and self-assessment worksheets.

The end-of-chapter assessment task in the *Student Book* provides formative assessment. Supporting materials for the assessment task can be found on the *Islam Kerboodle*, such as the Assessment Task Presentation and the related worksheets.

There are other opportunities for assessment too. For example, you could use some of the activities or reflection points throughout each *Student Book* unit, or some of the 'Further Suggestions' at the end of this chapter.

Getting ready for this chapter

- Buy a bag of fun-sized chocolate bars for Unit 4.1.
- You could invite key figures from the community or school community, e.g. a School Council Eco committee, to address the class about responsibility for the environment (Unit 4.5).
- Identify charities that students could raise money for.
- If you have the *Islam Kerboodle*, watch the case study film clips in advance, so that you can prepare and guide students before and during their viewing.

Objectives and outcomes for this chapter

Objectives	Unit	Outcomes
Most students will:		Most students will be able to:
• examine why life after death is important for Muslims • identify how Islamic belief in an afterlife influences their actions • reflect on what they think is the purpose of life.	4.1	• state Islamic beliefs about the purpose of life • explain why Muslims do good deeds • say what they think happens when we die.
• examine Islamic attitudes to death and bereavement • explain the concept of shirk • reflect on whether belief in an afterlife comforts people facing death.	4.2	• outline an Islamic funeral ritual • evaluate good and bad deeds • comment on how death makes them feel.
• analyse the belief held by some Muslims that life is a test • identify and explore the two meanings of jihad • reflect on what they do when they face difficulty.	4.3	• explain the daily struggle to be a good Muslim • define greater and lesser jihad • express an opinion about why humans face difficulties and how we should approach them.
• examine further the idea that for Muslims, life is a test • evaluate the idea that the acceptance of life as a test makes suffering easier to bear • consider whether we should accept suffering as part of life.	4.4	• describe two ways in which Allah tests Muslims • explain how putting faith in Allah comforts those who are suffering • debate whether an omnipotent, benevolent God would allow suffering.
• analyse the Islamic belief that we are responsible for both the planet and other people • explain the importance of compassion in Islam • evaluate how far we are responsible for each other.	4.5	• define khalifah • outline the work of an Islamic charity to explain why Muslims look after the planet and give to charity • demonstrate how far beyond themselves their sense of responsibility extends.
• examine Islamic views about creation theories and science • evaluate the Islamic belief that Allah is Creator • reflect on your own beliefs about religious and scientific explanations of creation.	4.6	• describe the creation story in Islam • give reasons for why Muslims think creation shows Allah • consider whether faith and science can work together.
• learn about and explain Islamic attitudes to killing • consider how and why war and capital punishment might be thought of as different to murder • evaluate arguments for and against the taking of a life.	4.7	• state Islamic views about killing • consider their own views about taking a life, and whether it should always be thought of as murder.

The unit in brief

This unit introduces the idea of the purpose of life and life after death. It uses a case study to explore why Muslims might change their behaviour to try to please Allah, in the hope of a better life when they die. Heaven and hell are mentioned and the Islamic idea of the body and spirit is shown in a diagram.

Key ideas

- Muslims believe that this life is a preparation for eternal life after death
- Eternal life can be spent in heaven or hell, depending on someone's actions in this life
- For Muslims, this life is much less important than the afterlife – it's worth making sacrifices and facing tests now, for the promise of an eternity in heaven
- Muslims believe that each person comprises a body and a spirit

Skills practised

- Thinking: considering the different aspects that make up a human
- Interpretation: looking at how heaven has been imagined; creating their own idea of heaven
- Reflection: reflecting on students' personal beliefs about the afterlife

Resources

- 4.1 Afterlife Film Clip: Sarrah and Ibrahim Yassin talk about their belief in life after death
- 4.1 Film Worksheet: students assess their understanding of the case study film clip by linking ideas to the *Student Book*
- 4.1 Afterlife Interactive Activity: students tick the statements which are true about the afterlife in Islam
- 4.1 Lesson Player: a ready-to-go presentation with built-in resources and teacher notes
- 4 Image Gallery: a useful gallery of photos and film stills from the chapter
- 4.1 Self-Assessment Sheet: students evaluate their learning against the lesson objectives

Ideas for starters

1. Use the Starter from the *Student Book*. Extend the activity by holding a class debate: 'Does being good just to get something make us better people?'

2. Ask students whether they remember a time when they made what they thought was a good decision, but in hindsight it would have been better to have let someone else be in charge. Ask them to share in groups and then feed back as a class.

3. Show a range of advertisements using 'heaven' as a theme. Discuss what advertising 'heaven' says about a product.

4. If you have the resources available, give students a small gift at the start of the lesson (e.g. a fun-sized chocolate bar), and tell them that they can eat it any time — but if they don't, they will get a reward. At the end of the lesson, award more chocolate (or house points) to those students who didn't eat their gifts, and discuss how hard it was to resist temptation.

Activity guidance

- You could follow up the idea of human decisions not being perfect (in Activity 1 of the *Student Book*), by asking whether students know of any historical decisions made by humans that, with hindsight, have not been good (cross-curricular).

Ideas for plenaries

1. Use the Reflection from the *Student Book*.

2. Ask students what good things they would be prepared to sacrifice in this life in order to secure eternal life. Allow them the opportunity to say if they would rather not live forever, and why.

3. Ask students to create a travel advertisement for a trip to heaven. Tell them that they must include: who can go, what the visitors need to take with them, and what it will cost them to go.

Further class and homework activities

1. Ask students to explore possible answers to the following question with a partner: should you do good to get to heaven, or because it's right to do good?

2. 4.1 Afterlife Film Clip and the accompanying 4.1 Film Worksheet on the *Islam Kerboodle*.

3. 4.1 Afterlife Interactive Activity on the *Islam Kerboodle*.

4. Further suggestions on page 76 of this book.

The unit in brief

This unit looks at Islamic attitudes to death and bereavement, starting with the idea of death as the beginning of the afterlife. Judgement is related to both actions and intentions. Rituals around death are outlined, together with support for the bereaved.

Key ideas

- Muslims believe that people will be judged on their death according to their deeds in life
- Many also believe that there is an angel constantly on each shoulder – one recording good deeds and one recording bad
- Believing in something other than Allah at the time of death, or saying that Allah has an equal, is the worst sin – called shirk
- Muslims give a lot of support to bereaved people, both in praying and reading the Qur'an with them, and also practically

Skills practised

- Reflection: reflecting on students' own actions using a weighing scale diagram
- Thinking: considering 'shirk' and what actions it might refer to
- Interpretation: looking at what happens when a Muslim dies, and interpreting the actions according to various Islamic beliefs

Resources

- 4.2 Audio Clip: a recording of an Islamic funeral prayer
- 4.2 Attitudes to Death Worksheet: a sorting activity about Islamic funeral rites
- 4.2 Attitudes to Death Interactive Activity: students complete sentences about Islamic beliefs about death
- 4.2 Lesson Player: a ready-to-go presentation with built-in resources and teacher notes
- 4 Image Gallery: a useful gallery of photos and film stills from the chapter
- 4.2 Self-Assessment Sheet: students evaluate their learning against the lesson objectives

Ideas for starters

1. Use the Starter from the *Student Book*.

2. Show a picture of the atomic mushroom cloud at Hiroshima or Nagasaki. Ask students whether a bad deed with a good intention deserves punishment. Then show a picture of a famous celebrity raising money for charity. Ask students whether the celebrity's motives will always be good (e.g. they might be doing it for publicity to improve their image).

Activity guidance:

- Activity 1 in the *Student Book* allows students to reflect on the idea that it's the balance of actions that is judged. You might want to emphasize to students that Muslims believe Allah is merciful and wants people to pass the tests set.

- The Reflection in the *Student Book* may cause some difficulties for students who have suffered bereavement, so you might want to suggest an appropriate alternative.

- You could compare Islamic beliefs about death with those of other faiths. For example, the Hindu idea of moksha and reincarnation, or the Christian idea of being 'saved by grace'. See Unit 1.3 in the *Hinduism Student Book* or Units 2.5 and 2.6 in the *Christianity Student Book*.

Ideas for plenaries

1. Use the Reflection from the *Student Book*.

2. Give students a blank grid, like the one below, to record their feelings, thoughts and images associated with the Reflection:

Feelings and thoughts about it; images or pictures in mind	Before	After

3. Conduct a think, pair, share activity. Ask students: 'Why is support from the jama'ah important to Muslims at the time of bereavement?'

Further class and homework activities

1. The flow-diagram activity in the *Student Book* could form the basis for a homework. Ask students to choose a particular Islamic burial practice, and make notes about what that particular action might mean in the context of wider Islamic beliefs.

2. 4.2 Attitudes to Death Worksheet on the *Islam Kerboodle*.

3. 4.2 Attitudes to Death Interactive Activity on the *Islam Kerboodle*.

4. Further suggestions on page 76 of this book.

The unit in brief

This unit outlines the differences between lesser and greater jihad. The lesson focuses first on the greater jihad, with a case study of young Muslims talking about their own personal struggles.

The lesser jihad (holy war/struggle) is then introduced, and students are invited to engage with questions about why there are negative perceptions of Muslims in the news.

Key ideas

- Some Muslims believe that life is a test
- The greater jihad is the personal struggle to be a good Muslim when being tested
- The lesser jihad is holy war/struggle
- Islam forbids terrorism, but a very small minority of Muslims believe that they are fighting a 'holy war' when committing these acts

Skills practised

- Empathy: considering the possible impacts of the idea that life is like a test on a young Muslim
- Thinking: considering reasons why one type of jihad is believed to be 'greater'
- Communication: discussing possible reasons for negative perceptions of Islam in the media, and what Muslims could do to challenge those perceptions
- Reflection: reflecting on personal struggles to do the right thing

Resources

- 4.3 Jihad Film Clip A: Rahaf and Saad Ahmed talk about their belief that life is a test
- 4.3 Jihad Film Clip B: Rahaf and Saad Ahmed talk about why Allah might want to test them
- 4.3 Film Worksheet: students assess their understanding of the case study film clips by linking ideas to the *Student Book*
- 4.3 Lesson Player: a ready-to-go presentation with built-in resources and teacher notes
- 4.3 Jihad Interactive Activity: students fill the gaps in a paragraph about jihad
- 4 Image Gallery: a useful gallery of photos and film stills from the chapter
- 4.3 Self-Assessment Sheet: students evaluate their learning against the lesson objectives

Ideas for starters

1. Use the Starter from the *Student Book*.

2. Ask students to discuss with a friend the most difficult thing they have to do at home (e.g. a chore, being nice to their siblings, etc.). Ask whether they try to do it, and if so why.

3. Divide the class into groups. Then ask the groups to create freeze-frames depicting different challenges that a person might face in life.

4. Ask students to use words or images to create a 'scale of difficulty' for personal challenges – ranging from challenges like failing an exam to natural disasters.

Activity guidance

- You could build on Activity 1 in the *Student Book* by asking students to look at their findings in light of the Islamic concept that life is like a test. Ask what positive qualities they might develop during these challenges. Or do they think that there are some challenges in life which are just difficult and don't teach us anything?

- Some people feel that photo b should not be included in an RE book because it could give a false impression about Islamic beliefs on the meaning of jihad. Ask students to write a letter to the publisher presenting arguments either for or against including the photo. Ask them to ensure they back up their view with well researched evidence.

Ideas for plenaries

1. Use the Reflection from the *Student Book*.

2. Ask students, in pairs or threes, to explain (with their books closed) the difference between lesser and greater jihad.

3. Ask students to design the icon for a 'Daily Jihad' app for a smart phone, on the greater jihad. Students should use their learning to think about what symbol would sum up the content.

Further class and homework activities

1. As a homework activity, ask students to keep diaries of the various challenges they face before the next lesson. Tell them that their diaries should consider whether or not they think the challenge benefitted them at all.

2. 4.3 Jihad Film Clips A and B, and the accompanying 4.3 Film Worksheet, on the *Islam Kerboodle*.

3. As well as showing students 4.3 Film Clips A and B on the *Islam Kerboodle*, you could explore the issue of the perceptions that people have of Islam in the media, with reference to Unit 5.5.

4. 4.3 Jihad Interactive Activity on the *Islam Kerboodle*.

5. Further suggestions on page 76 of this book.

The unit in brief

This unit explains that, for Muslims, everything happens for a reason, because they believe Allah has a plan for everyone. It uses a case study to present different arguments put forward by Muslims to explain why people suffer, which students are invited to evaluate.

Key ideas

- Muslims believe that all life is a test from Allah and that they will be judged on their responses to it
- Islam teaches that Muslims should rely on their faith to get them through suffering, even when they can't see the big picture
- Some believe that good things can come from suffering, such as compassion and charity

Skills practised

- Thinking: applying arguments from this unit to a real-world example from the news
- Literacy: analysing a quotation from the Qur'an; writing a journal entry
- Problem-solving: evaluating reasons given for suffering
- Reflection: reflecting on personal experiences of suffering

Resources

- 4.4 Suffering Arguments Worksheet: students evaluate different arguments to do with suffering in a grid
- 4.4 Suffering Arguments Interactive Activity: students are guided through writing a response to the statement 'a good God wouldn't let people suffer for any reason'
- 4.4 Lesson Player: a ready-to-go presentation with built-in resources and teacher notes
- 4 Image Gallery: a useful gallery of photos and film stills from the chapter
- 4.4 Self-Assessment Sheet: students evaluate their learning against the lesson objectives

Ideas for starters

1. Use the Starter from the *Student Book*. Ask the class what they believe the biggest problems in the world are. They should consider the extent to which their suggestions are man-made or occur naturally. Ideas like global warming would allow exploration of the extent to which people are causing the planet's problems.

2. Show the class a variety of pictures of different types of suffering and ask students what they think the worst problem for mankind is.

3. Show the class pictures of the London riots taking place in August 2011. Then show them pictures of the local volunteers who came out the following day to help clear up the mess. Ask them whether, in general, they think there is more suffering or more goodness in the world.

Activity guidance

Use Unit 1.2 to refresh students' memories about the nature of Allah before conducting the debate in Activity 1 of the *Student Book*.

Ideas for plenaries

1. Use the Reflection from the *Student Book*.

2. Ask students to make a list of things that cause them to suffer in school. Then ask them whether any of the arguments in this unit have given them a different perspective, and how.

3. Ask students to choose an example of suffering in the world from the Starter activity. They then have to write a sympathetic postcard to someone who might be affected by it, incorporating the Islamic ideas from this unit.

Further class and homework activities

1. You could ask students to assess the levels they would give to each of the suffering arguments made in this unit. Then, ask them to write their own arguments, and peer-assess levels in pairs.

2. 4.4 Suffering Arguments Worksheet on the *Islam Kerboodle*.

3. 4.4 Suffering Arguments Interactive Activity on the *Islam Kerboodle*.

4. Further suggestions on page 76 of this book.

4.5 Are We Responsible? Khalifah for Muslims

The unit in brief

This unit looks at the responsibility that Muslims believe Allah has given to people for the planet, and those living on it. Topics covered include responsibility, use of natural resources, sharing of wealth and compassion for others.

Key ideas

- Muslims believe that the Earth is not 'owned' by humans, it was created by Allah
- Humans answer to Allah for their actions, and have a responsibility as stewards of the Earth
- Every individual is responsible for the planet, animals, natural environment and each other
- Resources should not be wasted – people should use only what they need and spare resources should be shared
- Compassion for others is essential

Skills practised

- Literacy: considering synonyms for stewardship
- Communication: presenting a one-minute speech on the biggest problem the world faces
- Reflection: reflecting on own actions in environmental issues, and responsibility for others

Resources

- 4.5 Steward Worksheet: students explore the meanings of words from a diagram in the *Student Book*
- 4.5 Khalifah Interactive Activity: students fill the gaps in a paragraph about Khalifah
- 4.5 Lesson Player: a ready-to-go presentation with built-in resources and teacher notes
- 4 Image Gallery: a useful gallery of photos and film stills from the chapter
- 4.5 Self-Assessment Sheet: students evaluate their learning against the lesson objectives

Ideas for starters

1. Use the Starter from the *Student Book*.

2. Have a list of common 'save the planet' ideas. Ask students which they did this week, e.g. switching off the lights, not having electronics on standby, recycling, not dropping litter, not leaving the tap running while cleaning their teeth, etc. This activity could be done in the form of a walking line:
   - All students should stand on one side of the room.
   - As you read out the ideas from your list, they should take a step forward if they did that thing in the last week.
   - See how many make it across the room.

Activity guidance

- Activity 2 in the *Student Book* could be completed by lining students up on a spectrum from 'Mostly driven by self-interest' to 'Mostly willing to put others first'. Students discuss with the person next to them and then pair up with someone from the opposite side of the spectrum.

- The one-minute speech (Activity 3 in the *Student Book*) could be delivered individually or in groups. If in groups, it might be fun to play 'just a minute', where they have to speak for a minute but can be buzzed by classmates who want to 'pause' the speech and ask questions.

Ideas for plenaries

1. Use the Reflection from the *Student Book*.

2. Ask students to make a khalifah promise. They should write down something that they will do this week and then swap with a classmate. Next lesson they can check each other's progress.

3. Start a problems and solutions board for the classroom – looking at the environment, e.g. solving the problem of litter in school or encouraging recycling.

4. Ask students to plan a project to raise funds for a water charity in an Islamic country, e.g. a cake sale.

Further class and homework activities

1. Ask students to debate the question: 'Why did Allah not share the Earth's resources more evenly amongst people?' They could begin by looking at it from the Islamic perspective (e.g. considering the idea that life is a test), before giving their own views.

2. 4.5 Steward Worksheet on the *Islam Kerboodle*.

3. 4.5 Khalifah Interactive Activity on the *Islam Kerboodle*.

4. Further suggestions on page 76 of this book.

The unit in brief

This unit considers Islamic views about creation and science. The creation story according to the Qur'an is outlined, alongside scientific explanations. A case study is used to show how Muslims view their faith in relation to science.

Key ideas

- Muslims believe that Allah is in charge of creation and created everything
- Many Muslims do not believe that science and faith are necessarily at odds
- Many Muslims believe that science is good and that it asks more and more questions that reveal the glory of Allah

Skills practised

- Thinking: critical analysis of scripture
- Evaluation: evaluating different theories about the origins of the universe
- Reflection: considering whether theories from science and faith can work together

Resources

- 4.6 Science Film Clip A: Mr and Mrs Atcha explain how science is linked with their faith
- 4.6 Science Film Clip B: Mrs Atcha talks about how science is encouraged in their family
- 4.6 Audio Clip: a recording of the Islamic creation story from the *Student Book*
- 4.6 Film Worksheet: students assess their understanding of the case study film clips by linking ideas to the *Student Book*
- 4.6 Creation Interactive Activity: students sort statements for and against faith and science working together
- 4.6 Lesson Player: a ready-to-go presentation with built-in resources and teacher notes
- 4 Image Gallery: a useful gallery of photos and film stills from the chapter
- 4.6 Self-Assessment Sheet: students evaluate their learning against the lesson objectives

Ideas for starters

1. Use the Starter from the *Student Book*. You could follow this up by asking students who they think would care about how life began. Ask whether they know of any theories about how the universe began.

2. Ask students whether there is anything that they 'know' to be true. Ask what it is that makes them so sure.

3. Ask the class, in groups, to play consequences backwards. One student writes a consequence on a piece of paper, followed by 'because', and the next student answers the 'because' with a new consequence. This continues until the final point becomes unanswerable.

Activity guidance

•   When students read about creationists, you might want to explain that there is in Islam, as in any faith, a range of views from those who would argue that stories from scripture are literal and accurate accounts of events, to those who do not concern themselves with exactly how things might have happened.

•   Activity 1 in the *Student Book* could be followed up with questions about whether evil and suffering are part of creation. Students could be given the option to create a collage that contradicts the original statement.

•   You may wish to explain to students that, in passages from the Qur'an, 'We' is often used when Allah is speaking. Clarify that Muslims believe in only one God.

Ideas for plenaries

1. Use the Reflection from the *Student Book*.

2. Ask students to vote with their feet. They should go to either the 'faith' side or the 'science' side and give a question they think their side can answer about creation.

3. Before being allowed to leave the lesson, students must choose a theory about the origins of the universe and give one reason why it might be thought of as convincing.

Further class and homework activities

1. 4.6 Science Films Clips A and B, and the accompanying 4.6 Film Worksheet, on the *Islam Kerboodle*.

2. 4.6 Creation Interactive Activity on the *Islam Kerboodle*.

3. Further suggestions on page 76 of this book.

4.7 Is Killing Ever Justified? War and Capital Punishment

The unit in brief

This unit looks at the issue of killing in Islam, focusing on capital punishment and war. It starts with a quotation from the Qur'an indicating that people should not be killed without a 'just' cause, and then looks at how this is applied in different situations.

Key ideas

- The Qur'an forbids killing, except for a 'just cause'
- Many Muslims believe that capital punishment is one possible 'just cause', but there are limitations in place
- Killing in war is known as the 'lesser jihad' and there are strict conditions which must be met for a conflict to be considered a 'just' war

Skills practised

- Literacy: writing big ideas succinctly in an acrostic poem
- Thinking: considering whether there is a 'just cause' when it comes to killing, and if so what it might be
- Reflection: considering students' own guiding principles for this topic

Resources

- 📄 4.7 Attitudes to Killing Worksheet: students complete written responses based on passages from the Qur'an

- 🖱 4.7 Attitudes to Killing Interactive Activity: students fill the gaps in a paragraph about Islamic attitudes to killing

- 🎓 4.7 Lesson Player: a ready-to-go presentation with built-in resources and teacher notes

- 🖥 4 Image Gallery: a useful gallery of photos and film stills from the chapter

- 📄 4.7 Self-Assessment Sheet: students evaluate their learning against the lesson objectives

Ideas for starters

1. Use the Starter from the *Student Book*.

2. Ask students to line up along a continuum line from 'It is never right to kill', through to 'Killing is sometimes justified'. They should then pair up on the line and discuss reasons why they placed themselves as they did.

3. Focus on one issue in the unit (capital punishment or war) and ask students to write word associations. From what they already know about Islam, how do they think a Muslim would feel about this issue?

Activity guidance

- Activity 1 in the *Student Book* acts as a reminder to students that Muslims believe peace is at the centre of Islam.

- Activity 2 in the *Student Book* may bring in ideas about jihad from Unit 4.3. This is a good way to assess students' understanding of jihad. This activity could also be performed as a role-play, if more suitable for the class.

- Islam can sometimes be seen as a harsh religion with severe punishments. It would be useful to discuss deterrence as an aim of punishment, and this could be linked to the importance of the ummah.

- The Reflection in the *Student Book* could be completed individually or as paired work. It is designed to raise the idea of principles as a guide for life, not just rules. It may be necessary as an introduction to this activity to explain again what a principle is – a rule that can be applied to more than one circumstance. This will help students to understand how Muslims should interpret religious teachings by going back to basic ideas.

Ideas for plenaries

1. Use the Reflection from the *Student Book*.

2. Ask students to choose one of the topics explored in this unit (capital punishment or war) and explain Islamic attitudes to it in no more than 15 words.

3. Thumb vote: is capital punishment wrong? Explain to a partner.

Further class and homework activities

1. Ask students to look again at the quotations from the Qur'an in Unit 4.7 of the *Student Book*. They should then create a word cloud with words showing what these ethical guidelines say about Islamic beliefs about Allah.

2. 4.7 Attitudes to Killing Worksheet on the *Islam Kerboodle*.

3. 4.7 Attitudes to Killing Interactive Activity on the *Islam Kerboodle*.

4. Further suggestions on page 76 of this book.

Chapter 4 Further Suggestions

These suggestions are addressed directly to students.

4.1 Do You Live For the Afterlife?

1 Make a word picture of either heaven or hell. Include all the things you think would go to each place. *

2 Make a list of the questions you would like to ask a prisoner on death row about their ideas of heaven and hell. Swap your list of questions with a partner and try to answer each other's. **

3 Debate the statement: 'It is better to live a good life out of respect for others, rather than living a good life because you fear going to hell.' ***

4.2 Death – the End or the Beginning?

1 Research the achievements so far of a famous Muslim, e.g. Muhammad Ali, Mo Farah, Malala Yousafzai, Yusuf Islam. Write what you think would be included in a newspaper or magazine article which reflects on their life written for a Muslim audience. *

2 Imagine that you were going to pay your respects to a recently bereaved Muslim family. Prepare what you would say to them. Give reasons. **

3 Research funeral practices in another faith, in order to find similarities and differences with those in Islam. How do you explain the differences? ***

4.3 Is Life a Test? The Two Types of Jihad

1 Make a diary of your day, showing where self-control was easy and hard. *

2 Everybody in the class should take a sticky note on which to write a challenge for someone else. The class should then mingle and place their sticky notes on each other's backs. When all of the notes have been placed, remove the ones from your back and decide whether or not the class has picked your biggest challenges. *

3 Write a letter to the editor of a newspaper who has presented an inaccurate view of jihad. Explain what jihad means to Muslims, and make recommendations about how the topic should be approached in the media. ***

4.4 How Can We Live With Suffering?

1 Read a book or watch a film about someone who has found themselves in a life-threatening situation, such as *Touching the Void* by Joe Simpson. Why do some people turn to God when they think their life is about to end? Discuss this in pairs. *

2 Reflect on your weaknesses. Then imagine that someone wants to test you to make you stronger. What sort of test would you expect? **

3 Debate the statement: 'Any suffering is a test, whether it's a small thing, like losing a mobile phone, or a big disaster like an earthquake.' ***

4.5 Are We Responsible? Khalifah for Muslims

1 Explain khalifah to the person or council responsible for the environment in your school, and suggest how they might use the idea to improve their plans for the school. Or, if there is no environmental rep, prepare an assembly on khalifah and include three ideas that everyone could do. **

2 Produce an appeal for necessities for a refugee family (mum, dad and two children). What are the minimum furniture requirements and other items they would need? *

3 What is the difference between what you have and what you think the refugee family above would need? Discuss in pairs the arguments for and against being able to buy anything you both need and want. ***

4.6 Does it Matter How the World was Created?

1 Make a collage of pictures of Islamic art showing creation. *

2 Research Islamic inventions to see how human creativity has benefitted humanity. Then present your findings to the class. *

3 Outline a plan to your teacher for a joint project between the Science department and RE to look at Darwinism and creationism. Which speakers would you invite and why? What questions would you ask them? **

4 Design a project to work with the Art and/or Music/Drama departments to create an installation in the school hall, or a dance performance, to reflect the debate between science and religion. ***

4.7 Is Killing Ever Justified? War and Capital Punishment

1 Research what British law says about killing in self-defence. Find recent newspaper coverage of examples of it. Make notes in your research about what a Muslim might say, and whether or not you think this is acceptable. **

2 Debate the statement: 'If more mercy is shown, behaviour would improve.' ***

3 Find the other conditions of jihad. Evaluate whether there are any jihad wars in the world right now. ***

Chapter 4 Assessment

Assessment in the *Student Book*

You will find an assessment task at the end of every chapter which focuses on AT2. In this chapter, the task asks students to produce a draft for a web page or social networking profile page which shows their philosophy of existence, and how this relates to Islamic beliefs.

In the *Student Book* (and on the supporting worksheets), you'll find guidance about levels of assessment that you can use to help your students understand what their work should include. You could ask them to use these criteria for self-or peer-assessment once they've completed the task.

Assessment Task for Chapter 4 (pages **62–63** of the *Islam Student Book*)

Objectives	Task
• Interpret Islamic teachings about the purpose and meaning of life • Demonstrate empathy with Islamic views • Reflect on your place and responsibility in the world	'My place in the world.' Produce a draft for a web page or social networking profile page to show your philosophy about your existence – where you came from, why you are here, and how you relate to the world around you. **a** Prepare: Using the ideas presented in Chapter 4, find key quotations and phrases that raise issues you would like to cover. **b** Reflect: Use the above ideas as a mirror to reflect your own views, by deciding to what extent you agree or disagree with them. **c** Create: Use your preparation to design a web page.

Assessment in *Kerboodle*

On the *Islam Kerboodle*, you'll find resources to use when introducing the assessment task to the class.

You can use the *Chapter 4 Assessment Task Presentation* as a front-of-class tool to help your students unpack the assessment criteria, and understand what is expected of them.

Chapter 4 Assessment Worksheets accompany the task, so that once you finish the presentation, your students can easily get started.

Auto-marked tests

The *Islam Kerboodle* also contains auto-marked tests for each chapter to help save you time setting questions and marking for AT1. The test for this chapter contains 15 questions and will take most students about half an hour. Test results are automatically stored in the markbook.

Digital markbook

A markbook and a reporting function complete the *Kerboodle* assessment package, so you can keep all your students' test results and assessment scores in one place. This can include the auto-marked tests as well as pieces of work you or the students have marked by hand.

▲ Assessment resources for Chapter 4 on the *Islam Kerboodle*

Chapter 5 Overview
Islamic Beliefs in Action

Helping you deliver Key Stage 3 RE

This chapter addresses the following areas of the Programme of Study:

Key concepts

Practices and ways of life

- Exploring the impact of religions and beliefs on how people live their lives
- Understanding that religious practices are diverse and are influenced by cultures

Identity, diversity and belonging

- Exploring the variety, difference and relationships that exist within and between religions, values and beliefs

Key processes

Learning about religion

- Investigate the impact of religious beliefs and teachings on individuals, communities and societies, the reasons for commitment and the causes of diversity
- Evaluate how religious beliefs and teachings inform answers to ultimate questions and ethical issues

Learning from religion

- Reflect on the relationship between beliefs, teachings, world issues and ultimate questions
- Evaluate beliefs, commitments and the impact of religion in the contemporary world
- Express insights into the significance and value of religion and other world views for human relationships personally, locally and globally

The big picture

These are the key ideas behind this chapter:

- British Muslims seek to combine a life of submission to Allah's will with a normal life in Britain.
- There are some things in British culture that British Muslims would not take part in, particularly forms of socializing, but most Muslims feel 'British'.
- In Islam, men and women have different responsibilities but are considered equal.
- Muslims value family, which includes the worldwide Islamic community, or ummah.

- The Qur'an gives guidance about ethical issues.
- Stereotypes and Islamophobia can be broken down by increased understanding of Islamic culture.

Chapter outline

Use this to give students a mental road map of the chapter:

5.1 Being a British Muslim – looks at what it means to be a British Muslim and how they link their British identity and faith

5.2 Same Difference? Men and Women in Islam – considers the rights and duties of men and women in Islam, and the view that they were created equal but different

5.3 Nature or Nurture? The Muslim Family – looks at the Islamic attitude to the family, and how difficult it can be to live a close family life in modern society

5.4 How Do We Know What Is Right? – introduces core beliefs and quotations from the Qur'an which form the basis for moral decision-making in Islam

5.5 Knowing and Understanding: Islam in the Media – introduces the concept of Islamophobia and examines how Muslims are portrayed in the media

5.6 We Have Given to You Each a Path – explores how Muslims view members of other faiths

Opportunities for assessment

Summative assessments on the *Islam Kerboodle* include auto-marked tests, interactive activities and self-assessment worksheets.

The end-of-chapter assessment task in the *Student Book* provides formative assessment. Supporting materials for the assessment task can be found on the *Islam Kerboodle*, such as the Assessment Task Presentation and the related worksheets.

There are other opportunities for assessment too. For example, you could use some of the activities or reflection points throughout each *Student Book* unit, or some of the 'Further Suggestions' at the end of this chapter.

Getting ready for this chapter

- For Unit 5.1, prepare a map of the town centre (or photocopy a simple map), for students who work more slowly.
- Gather sample letters to columnists to demonstrate the genre in Unit 5.3.
- Gather clippings of ethical dilemmas from the media for Unit 5.4.
- If you have the *Islam Kerboodle*, watch the case study film clips in advance, so that you can prepare and guide students before and during their viewing.

Objectives and outcomes for this chapter

Objectives	Unit	Outcomes
Most students will:		Most students will be able to:
• explain what it means to be a British Muslim • develop an understanding about how British Muslims link their identity and religion • reflect on what 'British' means to them.	5.1	• give examples of what the case study Muslims believe to be British • give examples of British things that Muslims do, including keeping the law • say whether it is important to feel British.
• evaluate the rights and duties of men and women in Islam • analyse the Islamic belief that Allah created men and women equal but different • reflect on whether society stereotypes people by gender.	5.2	• list the duties of men and women in Islam • debate whether they think society values men more than women, presenting reasoned arguments.
• learn about and explain the Islamic attitude to the family • evaluate how Muslims respond to the challenges faced by families in modern society • reflect on whether these values should apply to everyone.	5.3	• outline the Islamic attitude to the family, including towards the wider ummah • identify two problems of modern life and how they may be overcome • explain how certain values may help a community.
• learn why Muslims believe that life is special and sacred • explain how this influences Muslims when making decisions • reflect on who or what they turn to for ethical decisions.	5.4	• give examples from the Qur'an to support the view that Allah created life • explain how a Muslim might view a person with a low quality of life • express their own beliefs on creation and whether life has value.
• explore the perceptions of Islam in the media • examine what Muslims think about how they are shown in the media • reflect on why stereotypes sometimes exist.	5.5	• give examples of the ways in which the media represents Muslims • outline a story from the case studies about how Muslims react to this • describe a situation when they have stereotyped someone.
• explore how Islam regards other faiths • examine the values that Islam shares with other faiths • reflect on the benefits of having many friends from different backgrounds.	5.6	• write the Qur'an 5:48 in their own words • present values from Islam that are shared by the Abrahamic faiths • explain the advantages of having friends with different viewpoints.

The unit in brief

This unit looks at what it means to be a British Muslim, including Muslims who have lived in Britain their whole lives, and those who have converted to Islam and are not part of Muslim families. Using case studies, the concept of maintaining faith whilst living in Britain is explored.

Key ideas

- Roughly 4.6% of people in Britain are Muslim
- Being British means making your home in Britain, being part of the community, following British law, and looking after the country
- Muslims submit their life to Allah, which means following laws that prevent them from doing some of the things that many British people do, like drinking alcohol

Skills practised

- Literacy: creating a guide for a Muslim visitor
- Thinking: considering how easy it is to be spiritual in modern society
- Empathy: looking at the lives of British Muslims and identifying with them
- Reflection: reflecting on the importance of the need to feel 'British'

Resources

- 5.1 British Muslim Film Clip A: Mrs Atcha talks about how the public regard her as a Muslim
- 5.1 British Muslim Film Clip B: the Atcha family talks about their experiences of being Muslims in Britain
- 5.1 British Muslim Film Clip C: the Atcha family talks about what it means to be a Muslim in Britain
- 5.1 Film Worksheet: students assess their understanding of the case study film clips by linking ideas to the *Student Book*
- 5.1 British Muslim Interactive Activity: students sort statements according to whether they are challenges or advantages of being a Muslim in Britain
- 5.1 Lesson Player: a ready-to-go presentation with built-in resources and teacher notes
- 5 Image Gallery: a useful gallery of photos and film stills from the chapter
- 5.1 Self-Assessment Sheet: students evaluate their learning against the lesson objectives

Ideas for starters

1. Use the Starter from the *Student Book*. Asking students what it means to be British will enable them to identify common features of British culture. These can then be compared with the statements from Muslims to enable students to see common elements and differences.

2. Ask students whether they would describe themselves as British, and then explore where their families came from in previous generations.

3. Provide a selection of appropriate newspapers and magazines and ask students to create a collage about what it means to be British.

Activity guidance

*   Activity 1 in the *Student Book* will allow students to demonstrate knowledge from previous units, such as food, dress, etc. This activity could be done as a creative exercise – building a street as a class – or in conjunction with other subjects as a technical drawing or art project.

*   Activity 2 in the *Student Book* should feature culture rather than just food, dress, etc. Students may be prompted by the information in the case study quotations.

*   Activity 3 in the *Student Book* could be preceded by a meditation, focusing afterwards on how difficult it was to get everyday thoughts out of students' heads as they sat quietly.

Ideas for plenaries

1. Use the Reflection from the *Student Book* to discuss not only whether students think it's important that they feel British, but also whether British Muslims should be regarded as Muslim first or British first.

2. Ask students to role-play how they would welcome a new Muslim friend, e.g. at school, on a shopping trip, at a birthday party, at work, at a wedding, at a fundraising event.

Further class and homework activities

1. As a Starter, you could use 5 Image Gallery on the *Islam Kerboodle* to show students the image of the Queen of England or James Bond. Ask: 'What exactly is it that makes this person "British"? Why have they become a British symbol?'

2. 5.1 British Muslim Film Clips A, B and C, and the accompanying 5.1 Film Worksheet, on the *Islam Kerboodle*.

3. 5.1 British Muslim Interactive Activity on the *Islam Kerboodle*.

4. Further suggestions on page 92 of this book.

The unit in brief

This unit considers the rights and duties of men and women in Islam, and the Islamic belief that men and women were created equal but different. Original source material is used to explain this idea, and the complementary nature of men and women is also outlined.

Key ideas

- The Prophet Muhammad made it clear during his lifetime that women were equal to men
- In religious terms, the Qur'an sets out the same duties for men and women, and this is emphasized by the way that this was revealed
- Many Muslims believe that men and women were designed by Allah to complement each other and work together in partnership
- In the Qur'an, Muslim men and women have different responsibilities, although in practice this can be interpreted differently

Skills practised

- Literacy: analysing an original text and reflecting on certain features
- Thinking: considering interesting questions about male and female roles which could be put to a Muslim couple
- Reflection: reflecting on roles and responsibilities within students' own families

Resources

- 5.2 Audio Clip: a recording of the Qur'an 33:35 from the *Student Book*
- 5.2 Roles Worksheet: students complete a summary diagram about gender roles in Islam
- 5.2 Gender Interactive Activity: students read statements about men and women in Islam and decide which ones are true
- 5.2 Lesson Player: a ready-to-go presentation with built-in resources and teacher notes
- 5 Image Gallery: a useful gallery of photos and film stills from the chapter
- 5.2 Self-Assessment Sheet: students evaluate their learning against the lesson objectives

Ideas for starters

1. Use the Starter from the *Student Book*. Asking students what they think of when someone says 'Muslim woman' might bring out a variety of ideas – including questions about modesty, and whether Muslim women are controlled by men.

2. Ask students to role-play how chores are divided at home.

3. Ask students whether they think men and women are equal in Britain, and why.

Activity guidance

*   Writing questions to ask Mr and Mrs Atcha gives students the opportunity to be curious, and to express what they have noticed in the media or in the world around them. (You might also want to refer them to Unit 5.5.)

*   Activity 3 in the *Student Book* could be linked up explicitly with the work done in Unit 5.1 about British culture. Prompts could be given from the text. If Religious Studies is being taught alongside PSHE, it might be useful at this point to bring in magazines and analyse the suggested roles of men and women. Encourage students to analyse critically what they see.

Ideas for plenaries

1. Use the Reflection from the *Student Book*.

2. Use Activity 3 in the *Student Book* for a mini exit poll. Issue sticky notes or slips of paper that can be put into a box. Analyse the results next lesson.

3. Ask students to name two things that a woman is responsible for in Islam, and then two things that a man is responsible for. (You might want to clarify that many Muslims interpret these responsibilities in different ways.)

Further class and homework activities

1. 5.2 Roles Worksheet on the *Islam Kerboodle*.

2. 5.2 Gender Interactive Activity on the *Islam Kerboodle*.

3. Further suggestions on page 92 of this book.

The unit in brief

This unit looks at the Islamic attitude to the family. It considers, in particular, those issues that British Muslims may face as they try to live the Islamic life and bring up their families within broader British society.

Key ideas

- Family life is very important to Muslims, and this is supported through Islamic laws and Sunnah
- The Islamic view of 'family' is very broad – in fact, it can be used to refer to all Muslims worldwide
- Modern British society can sometimes provide challenges for Muslim families when they try to meet certain aims

Skills practised

- Literacy: creating a letter to an advice column based on table information
- Problem-solving: applying advice in a quotation to Muslim family life today
- Thinking: analysing a photograph
- Reflection: considering the role of prayer in family life

Resources

- 5.3 Muslim Family Worksheet: students complete a table based on the table in the *Student Book*
- 5.3 Muslim Family Interactive Activity: students decide whether statements about the Muslim family are true or false
- 5.3 Lesson Player: a ready-to-go presentation with built-in resources and teacher notes
- 5 Image Gallery: a useful gallery of photos and film stills from the chapter
- 5.3 Self-Assessment Sheet: students evaluate their learning against the lesson objectives

Ideas for starters

1. Use the Starter from the *Student Book*. As some students may not have a family unit, encourage them to think of guardians, friends and wider family too.

2. Ask students what the difference is between the words 'family' and 'fam'. Fam is used in the street sense of the word – derived from the word 'family' – referring to people who are extremely close (as if a family member). You could also use the street term 'blud'.

3. In groups, role-play one thing that might encourage a family to become closer, and one thing that might challenge them.

Activity guidance

- Activity 1 in the *Student Book* could be left to student choice, or the different problems could be divided up more formally between the students, so that all are covered. For higher ability students, the funeral rituals question offers an opportunity for extension. The relationships issue might be a good opportunity for extension homework.

- You may wish to compare this Unit with Units 5.2 and 5.3 in the *Christianity Student Book*.

Ideas for plenaries

1. Use the Reflection from the *Student Book* and discuss it as a class.

2. Ask students to rank the seven aims in the *Student Book* table, with the one they think of as most important at the top. Ask them to explain their reasoning.

3. Divide the class into three groups. A student from the first group should call out a family aim. A student from the second group should then give an example or examples of why this aim could be difficult. Finally, a student from the third group should give a possible solution that might help an Islamic family meet that aim.

4. Ask students to write in their planner one thing that they will do to make their family life better this week.

Further class and homework activities

1. As an extra class activity, ask students to plan a presentation for the new Year 7 students that outlines any community values and expectations that your school has, or should have.

2. 5.3 Muslim Family Worksheet on the *Islam Kerboodle*.

3. 5.3 Muslim Family Interactive Activity on the *Islam Kerboodle*.

4. Further suggestions on page 92 of this book.

The unit in brief

This unit introduces core beliefs and quotations from the Qur'an, which form the basis of moral decision-making in Islam. It also looks briefly at ethical dilemmas regarding the sacredness of life, and the role of the conscience or inner voice.

Key ideas

- The Qur'an gives guidance that can be applied to ethical problems. This is often the starting point when Muslims make decisions
- Relevant, general guidance can be found on various topics, even if they are not explicitly covered in the scriptures
- Many Muslims believe that ethical dilemmas are a test
- Muslims believe people have a conscience or inner voice to help them make the right decisions

Skills practised

- Literacy: evaluating original quotations and statements
- Thinking: considering a modern story about euthanasia
- Reflection: reflecting on students' own ethical decision-making processes

Resources

- 📄 5.4 Right or Wrong Worksheet: students analyse some quotations from the Qur'an and how they might help a Muslim decide what is right or wrong
- 🖱 5.4 Ethical Decisions Interactive Activity: students complete sentences about how Muslims are guided when making ethical decisions
- 🎓 5.4 Lesson Player: a ready-to-go presentation with built-in resources and teacher notes
- 🖥 5 Image Gallery: a useful gallery of photos and film stills from the chapter
- 📄 5.4 Self-Assessment Sheet: students evaluate their learning against the lesson objectives

Ideas for starters

1. Use the Starter from the *Student Book*.

2. As students enter the room, give each one a slip of paper with an ethical dilemma written on it. Tell them that they must decide what they think about their particular ethical dilemma and then mingle to find someone else in the class who shares their views. Possible ethical dilemmas could include:

- using science to help someone get pregnant
- having a blood transfusion
- donating your heart for transplant after you die
- using science to choose your baby's features
- cloning (making a replica of an animal or a person)
- experimenting on humans to create new drugs.

3. Ask students to form a continuum line, with 'Always listen to my conscience' at one end, and 'Highly value the influence of others' at the other. Ask students to comment on their choices.

Activity guidance

- In this unit, students are not expected to understand all of the issues, but the aim is rather that they should take away from this an understanding of how a Muslim would make decisions about ethical matters. You may wish to compare how different faiths respond to medical ethics; see Unit 4.2 in the *Christianity Student Book* or Units 4.4 and 4.5 in the *Sikhism Student Book*.

- You might choose to use the diagram text on the left-hand page to explore the differences between law and principle.

- Activity 3 in the *Student Book* could also be explored in the form of a role-play – encouraging students to verbalize the inner dialogue that the conscience has.

Ideas for plenaries

1. Use the Reflection from the *Student Book*.

2. Ask students to line up against one wall and take a step forward every time they agree with a statement that you read out. Either use the ethical dilemmas from Starter 2 above, or ask students to generate suggestions by putting them into a suggestion box.

Further class and homework activities

1. Ask students to design a page-a-day desk calendar for one week (with tear-off pages) to remind a Muslim about right and wrong. They should choose seven statements for seven days this week and illustrate the calendar with Islamic designs.

2. 5.4 Right or Wrong Worksheet on the *Islam Kerboodle*.

3. 5.4 Ethical Decisions Interactive Activity on the *Islam Kerboodle*.

4. Further suggestions on page 92 of this book.

5.5 Knowing and Understanding: Islam in the Media

The unit in brief

This unit uses case study material to look at how Muslims are portrayed in the media, and what affect this can have on people's perceptions of them. It also introduces the concept of Islamophobia.

Key ideas

- As a result of negative media coverage, some Muslims are treated with suspicion or treated badly
- Stereotypes are not always helpful when it comes to real people
- Once people start to really communicate, stereotypes are often broken down

Useful Word

Islamophobia

Skills practised

- Literacy: working with a genre – 'letter to the editor' and newspaper front page
- Thinking: considering the role of newspapers in presenting a balanced view
- Reflection: reflecting on students' own experiences of stereotyping someone, and where those attitudes might come from

Resources

- 5.5 Media Film Clip A: Mr and Mrs Atcha talk about being Muslims in Britain
- 5.5 Media Film Clip B: Mrs Atcha talks about being a Muslim in Britain
- 5.5 Film Worksheet: students assess their understanding of the case study film clips by linking ideas to the *Student Book*
- 5.5 Media Interactive Activity: students fill the gaps in a paragraph about Islam in the media
- 5.5 Lesson Player: a ready-to-go presentation with built-in resources and teacher notes
- 5 Image Gallery: a useful gallery of photos and film stills from the chapter
- 5.5 Self-Assessment Sheet: students evaluate their learning against the lesson objectives

Ideas for starters

1. Use the Starter from the *Student Book*. Ask students: 'If someone is stereotyped for a positive quality, e.g. "Girls are good at multi-tasking", is this therefore a good thing?'

2. Show the class a range of media headlines (if possible, including examples which feature Islam) and ask students to analyse whether the headlines present a balanced view of the topic or person it refers to. Ask why or why not.

Activity guidance

- This unit could be set up as a whole project looking at the media and Muslims, with largely independent work. Students could be asked in advance to produce media cuttings and stories, or, if there is a subscription to an educational newspaper, students could search for relevant topics.

- Activity 2 in the *Student Book* could be a good homework activity, especially if students choose the topics beforehand.

Ideas for plenaries

1. Use the Reflection from the *Student Book*. This could be done as a think, pair, share activity.

2. Ask the whole class to submit ideas about how to promote a balanced view of Muslims to their community.

3. Ask students to write headlines that present a balanced view of Muslims.

Further class and homework activities

1. As a homework activity, ask students to produce a word picture showing why it can be unhelpful to stereotype Muslims. The word-picture format could link with Islamic art.

2. As a class activity, and useful whole-course reflection, ask students to produce a collage of quotations from the case studies throughout the *Student Book* that a media editor might find useful to help them understand what Muslims really think about different topics.

3. 5.5 Media Film Clips A and B, and the accompanying 5.5 Film Worksheet, on the *Islam Kerboodle*.

4. 5.5 Media Interactive Activity on the *Islam Kerboodle*.

5. Further suggestions on page 92 of this book.

The unit in brief

This unit uses case study quotations to introduce Muslims' relationships with people of other faiths. A quotation from the Qur'an suggests that Muslims see living amongst others as part of the test to remain faithful to Islam wherever they are.

Key ideas

- Many Muslims believe that it's important to have friends from different backgrounds and belief systems
- Some Muslims feel that they cannot do some of the things their friends do, because Muslims put their faith before all else
- The Qur'an encourages Muslims to be true to their own faith whatever their context

Skills practised

- Literacy: comprehension – looking at an extended quotation from scripture
- Interpretation: applying the quotation to a modern Muslim context
- Thinking: considering why faiths sometimes work together when there are big differences between them
- Reflection: thinking about the advantages of having friends with different viewpoints

Resources

- 5.6 Other Faiths Film Clip: the Atcha family talk about how they interact with people of different faiths
- 5.6 Audio Clip: a recording of the Qur'an 5:48 from the *Student Book*
- 5.6 Film Worksheet: students assess their understanding of the case study film clip by linking ideas to the *Student Book*
- 5.6 Other Faiths Interactive Activity: students sort statements according to whether they are advantages or disadvantages of different faiths interacting
- 5.6 Lesson Player: a ready-to-go presentation with built-in resources and teacher notes
- 5 Image Gallery: a useful gallery of photos and film stills from the chapter
- 5.6 Self-Assessment Sheet: students evaluate their learning against the lesson objectives

Ideas for starters

1. Use the Starter from the *Student Book*.

2. Ask students to walk round the room and, on a signal, pair up with somebody they are not already friends with. Their joint task is then to find three things that they have in common. When they return to their seats, they should consider which areas they looked at in order to find the three areas of commonality. Ask whether they considered each other's beliefs, or more everyday things.

Activity guidance

- Activity 1 in the *Student Book* could also be done as a role-play in groups, or a series of freeze-frames.

- Activity 2 in the *Student Book* could be extended if PSHE is being taught alongside RE. It could be emphasized that spending time with those who are different (including those with disabilities, other genders and ages, etc.) can increase understanding and empathy.

Ideas for plenaries

1. Use the Reflection from the *Student Book*.

2. Ask students to use just one word to summarize how their life would change if they had more friends with different belief systems.

3. Ask students, without showing anyone, to write down one Islamic value on a piece of paper. The class then mingle and students have to find somebody else who has written down the same value. Discuss how this could be built into a friendship.

Further class and homework activities

1. You could stretch some students by asking them to consider some of the issues that may arise between friends of different faiths. For example, they could find out more about what Muslims and Christians believe about Jesus (Isa), or holy texts.

2. 5.6 Other Faiths Film Clip, and the accompanying 5.6 Film Worksheet, on the *Islam Kerboodle*.

3. 5.6 Other Faiths Interactive Activity on the *Islam Kerboodle*.

4. Further suggestions on page 92 of this book.

Chapter 5 Further Suggestions

These suggestions are addressed directly to students.

5.1 Being a British Muslim

1   Research how popular TV programmes portray Muslims and present your findings to the class. Organize a letter to the channel if the class thinks they are unfairly stereotyping Muslims. *

2   Imagine you are the Human Resources Manager for a large employer. Write your company policy on how Muslims will be treated within your company. Think about questions like: 'Will Muslims be given time off to pray each day? What are they allowed to wear? What food and drink will your canteen offer?' **

5.2 Same Difference? Men and Women in Islam

1   Draw a Venn diagram with two circles. Put 'male characteristics' on one side and female on the other. How much do they overlap? *

2   Outline the responsibilities that you would give to your mother and father if you could decide how your family is organized. Give your reasons. *

3   Visit a book shop and research how many books there are to help men and women understand each other, e.g. *Men are from Mars, Women are from Venus*. Do you think the Qur'an should be included on these shelves? Why or why not? **

5.3 Nature or Nurture? The Muslim Family

1   Plan time with your grandparents or older relatives. What would you do to honour them? *

2   Research what Islamic charities do for the ummah. **

3   'It's fine to be single. We don't need anyone else to be happy.' How far do you agree? What might a Muslim argue?

5.4 How Do We Know What Is Right?

1   Use the phrase 'Allah does not send a soul more than it can bear', and design a poster that draws on your learning in this unit. If you can, include the Arabic lettering. On the back, write where you would like to display your poster – thinking about the people who might appreciate its message. **

2   Spend a day trying to 'tune in' to your 'inner voice', or conscience. Write a diary entry explaining whether you felt different, or acted in a way you might not have done otherwise. *

3   Research the work of NICE and see how decisions are made about the allocation of NHS resources. How might a Muslim want to influence this? Why? ***

5.5 Knowing and Understanding: Islam in the Media

1   Monitor the newspapers for a week. Highlight all references to Muslims and Islam. *

2   If you feel that coverage of Muslims from your research above is unfair, write a letter to the editor. **

3   Using your learning from this unit, along with your own reflections, write a letter to a Muslim advising them about how to deal with some of the attitudes they may face in Britain. ***

5.6 We Have Given to You Each a Path

1   Make a large artwork of Surah 5:48–49 from the *Student Book* for the wall of your classroom. Remember that, in Islamic art, the human form is not allowed, so use colour, shape and pattern to symbolize your ideas. **

2   Plan an outing for a group of mixed-faith friends. **

3   The Qur'an says that no matter what their religion, the leaders of each faith must lead their followers so as to avoid hypocrisy (saying they believe one thing but acting differently). Write a letter to the leader of any faith saying what their priorities should be for their followers in the twenty-first century. ***

Chapter 5 Assessment

Assessment in the *Student Book*

You will find an assessment task at the end of every chapter which focuses on AT2. In this chapter, the task asks students to imagine they are the mayor of their town, and they have been given the task of improving the facilities for Muslims by creating an action plan.

In the *Student Book* (and on the supporting worksheets), you'll find guidance about levels of assessment that you can use to help your students understand what their work should include. You could ask them to use these criteria for self- or peer-assessment once they've completed the task.

Living Faiths Assessment

Student Book
- Assessment Task
- Levels Guidance

Kerboodle
- Auto-Marked Test
- Assessment Task Presentation
- Assessment Worksheets

Assessment Task for Chapter 5 (pages **76–77** of the *Islam Student Book*)

Objectives
- Demonstrate knowledge of how Muslims apply rules in their lives
- Apply knowledge to designing facilities and services for Muslims and making sure their needs are met

Task
Imagine that you are the mayor of your town, and you have been given the task of improving the facilities for Muslims. Using what you've learned, produce an action plan for your town, with reasons to back up your suggestions. What new or improved facilities or services would be needed?

Assessment in *Kerboodle*

On the *Islam Kerboodle*, you'll find resources to use when introducing the assessment task to the class.

You can use the *Chapter 5 Assessment Task Presentation* as a front-of-class tool to help your students unpack the assessment criteria, and understand what is expected of them.

Chapter 5 Assessment Worksheets accompany the task, so that once you finish the presentation, your students can easily get started.

Auto-marked tests

The *Islam Kerboodle* also contains auto-marked tests for each chapter to help save you time setting questions and marking for AT1. The test for this chapter contains 15 questions and will take most students about half an hour. Test results are automatically stored in the markbook.

Digital markbook

A markbook and a reporting function complete the *Kerboodle* assessment package, so you can keep all your students' test results and assessment scores in one place. This can include the auto-marked tests as well as pieces of work you or the students have marked by hand.

▲ Assessment resources for Chapter 5 on the *Islam Kerboodle*

Glossary

Abrahamic faiths Those faiths (Islam, Judaism and Christianity) that acknowledge Abraham as a common origin

Adhan When a person called the Mu'adhin says a prayer calling Muslims to pray; in many countries it is played through loudspeakers from the minaret (tower) of a mosque, so that everyone can hear, stop what they are doing and pray

Akhirah Eternal life

Alhamdulillah Thanks be to Allah

Allah The Arabic name for God, used in Islam

Atheist A person who does not believe in the existence of any god

Capital punishment Killing/executing somebody, using a country's legal process, for a serious crime they have committed

Compassion Sympathizing with someone's situation with a desire to make it better

Du'a Personal prayer

Eid-ul-Adha Festival of sacrifice

Eid-ul-Fitr The celebration at the end of Ramadan, after a month of fasting

Euthanasia The act of killing someone painlessly, usually to end their suffering; this is illegal in Britain

Gospels The four books at the start of the New Testament in the Bible

Hadith The collected sayings of the Prophet Muhammad

Hajj The fifth pillar of Islam; a pilgrimage to Makkah that Muslims should try to complete at least once in their lives, if they are able

Halal Lawful

Haram Unlawful

Hijab Muslim woman's head, hair and chest covering

Idol worship The worship of statues, or things that are not God

Imam A religious leader in Islam

Inshaa Allah If God wills it

Islamophobia Prejudice against Muslims because of their religion, including a hatred of Islam that leads to fear and dislike of Muslims

Jama'ah Local mosque community of Muslims

Jihad Personal struggle (the 'greater' jihad); holy war or struggle (the 'lesser' jihad)

Ka'bah A cube-shaped structure in the centre of the grand mosque in Makkah; it does not contain anything to worship – in fact, Muhammad removed all 'idols' from it

Khalifah The idea that Allah made people responsible for the Earth

Khutbah Sermon at Friday prayers

Makkah The holiest city of Islam; Muslims face towards Makkah when they pray

Mercy Showing forgiveness to somebody who you could punish

Modesty Decency of behaviour, speech and dress

Mosque clothes Traditional clothes worn by some Muslim men for going to the mosque (an Islamic place of worship)

Persecution Hostility towards and ill treatment of an individual or group, often because of their race, religion or politics

Pilgrimage A special journey with spiritual intention

Polytheism Belief in more than one God

Qur'an The holy text in Islam

Quraysh A tribe in Makkah in Muhammad's lifetime

Qurbani The meat of animals sacrificed at Eid-ul-Adha that are shared with family and the poor

Ramadan The ninth month of the Islamic year; the time when the Qur'an was revealed to the Prophet Muhammad (and now the most holy month)

Revelation Revealing or showing communication from Allah

Righteousness Being moral or acting properly

Sadaqah Any good deed done for the sake of Allah, rather than selfish reasons

Salah The second pillar of Islam; Islamic prayer carried out five times each day

Sawm Fasting; going without food or drink from dawn to sunset

Secular Without religious reference; non-religious

Shahadah The words Muslims use to confirm their belief and to declare that they are Muslim

Shari'ah Islamic law derived by scholars from the Qur'an, Sunnah and Hadith

Shaytan Satan, or the devil

Shirk Believing in something other than Allah at the time of death, or saying that Allah has an equal

Subhah These are beads used to keep count of personal prayers. Some have 99 beads and some 33, so they are especially useful for reciting the 99 names of Allah

Sunnah Actions and teaching of the Prophet Muhammad

Tayyib Pure

The Night Journey A miraculous spiritual journey, during which the Prophet Muhammad was taken from Makkah to 'the farthest place of worship' (The Qur'an 17:1)

Ummah Worldwide community of Muslims

Zakah The third pillar of Islam; payment of 2.5% of annual savings

OXFORD
UNIVERSITY PRESS

Great Clarendon Street, Oxford, OX2 6DP, United Kingdom

Oxford University Press is a department of the University of Oxford.
It furthers the University's objective of excellence in research,
scholarship, and education by publishing worldwide. Oxford is a
registered trade mark of Oxford University Press in the UK and in
certain other countries

© Oxford University Press 2013

The moral rights of the author have been asserted

First published in 2013

British Library Cataloguing in Publication Data
Data available

978-0-19-913808-1

10 9 8 7 6 5 4 3 2

Paper used in the production of this book is a natural, recyclable
product made from wood grown in sustainable forests.
The manufacturing process conforms to the environmental regulations
of the country of origin.

Printed in Great Britain by Ashford Print and Publishing Services, Gosport

Acknowledgements

The publishers would like to thank the following for permissions to use their photographs:

Cover: Godong/Robert Harding/Rex Features; All other photos by OUP

From the author, Stella Neal: I would like to thank Mujtaba Nazir for his research contribution
and his guidance. I would also like to thank my two patient children, William and Elsie, who are
around the same age of the readers of this book. Without their love and support this would have
been impossible to achieve. Also to my Muslim friends who fed me, remained excited when I was
bogged down with hard work and reminded me that my duty was to please Allah with this book.
Finally, the experience that goes into this book has been gained by learning from the pupils I
teach at Slough Grammar School. Marshallah, their sharing and expression of love for Islam has
driven my curiosity as I hope it will yours.

OUP wishes to thank the Yassin, Ahmed and Atcha families for agreeing to take part in the case
study films and to be photographed for this title.

We are grateful for permission to reprint extracts from the following
copyright material:

Extracts from The Qu'ran are taken from the following translations:
The Qu'ran Sahih International version (Al Muntada al-Aslami, 2004)
The Qu'ran in English and Arabic translated by Yusuf Ali
(Sh Muhammad Aswat, 1975)
The Noble Quran translated by Dr Muhammad Muhsin Khan:
(Dar-us Salam Publications, 1994)

We are grateful for permission to reprint extracts from the following:

The Way of the Prophet: a Selection of Hadith by Abd Al-Ghaffar Hasan, translated and edited by
Usama Hasan (The Islamic Foundation, 2009), reprinted by permission of the publishers,
Kube Publishing Ltd.

Although we have made every effort to trace and contact all copyright
holders before publication this has not been possible in all cases.
If notified, the publisher will rectify any errors or omissions at the
earliest opportunity.

Links to third party websites are provided by Oxford in good faith
and for information only. Oxford disclaims any responsibility for the
materials contained in any third party website referenced in this work.